Introduction to

Residential Construction Lending

Prepared by

Trinity Performance Improvement

Introduction to Residential Construction Lending

Published by Trinity Real Estate Solutions®, Inc.
4851 LBJ Freeway, Suite 410
Dallas, TX 75244
www.trinityonline.com

This publication is designed to provide accurate and authoritative information regarding the subject matter covered. It is sold with the understanding that the publisher is not engaged in rendering legal or other professional services. If legal advice or other professional assistance is required, the services of a competent professional person should be sought.

Limits of Liability and Disclaimer of Warranty: While every precaution has been taken in preparing this book, including research, development and testing of each module, the Publisher and Author assume no responsibility for errors or omissions. No liability is assumed by either the Publisher or Author for damages resulting in the use of this information.

The modules within this book are based upon product information obtained as of June 2014. Due to the rapid changes in the construction/real estate/lending fields, it is possible that some differences exist between the information within the modules and the actual current processes.

ISBN 978-0-9909928-1-3

Printed in the United States of America
FIRST EDITION

Trademarks

All trademarks and trade names referred to in this publication are the property of the respective companies.
"Trinity Real Estate Solutions," "Trinity Appraisal Services," "Trinity Field Services," "Trinity Inspection Services," "Trinity Loan Administration," "Trinity Residential Land Services" and the stylized "T" logo are registered trademarks of Trinity Real Estate Solutions, Inc. © 2018

Documentation and Training

Trinity Real Estate Solutions, Inc. and subsidiaries Trinity Loan Administration, Trinity Inspection Services, Trinity Field Services, Trinity Appraisal Services and Trinity Residential Land Services are committed to continuously improving our training materials and documentation through our Performance Improvement team. Constructive feedback from our partners is welcomed. If you have any suggestions or comments, please send them to info@trinityonline.com.

Acknowledgements

Over the life of this book, many individuals assisted in this endeavor. To communicate the message accurately, effectively and thoroughly, a uniquely collective and specialized skill set is required. From inspiration to documentation to execution to distribution, numerous talented individuals were involved.

We sincerely thank those that contributed, corrected and reviewed this handbook. Without their efforts, this book would not be possible.

Brad Meyer
Carolyn Cameron
Chris Wood
Ed Massey
Jerry Sattler
Jim Adams
Peter Shriver

Other Books by Trinity Performance Improvement

Introduction to Residential Draw Inspections

Trinity Real Estate Solutions

Trinity Real Estate Solutions® operates as a national provider of construction lending services, offering specialty property inspections, loan administration services, consulting services and valuation analysis for residential, light commercial and business properties. Trinity's products are designed to protect customers' investments, mitigate risk, and provide onsite assessments of properties. By fully partnering with our customers, Trinity sets the standard for exceptional service while delivering industry-leading response times and ensuring our clients receive individualized support and customized services to meet all their needs.

Because of our extensive experience and broad network of field representatives, Trinity possesses the resources and experience for any residential and light commercial sized project in any location. Trinity's growth and continued success is attributed to our understanding of each customer's need for accurate and on-time information.

As a unified company serving customers in the banking, mortgage lending, insurance and credit card industries, Trinity functions as five interrelated but distinct companies:

Trinity Appraisal Services® LLC

▶ Provides a uniquely targeted range of new construction and renovation appraisal products and services. We operate as a nationwide trusted advisor to our customer's management team by offering unbiased guidance on critical lending decisions.

Trinity Field Services® LLC

▶ Acts as your eyes in the field for residential and commercial property site inspections. Trinity consistently sets ourselves apart by providing an unparalleled level of service, prompt order processing and comprehensive risk management.

Trinity Inspection Services® LLC

▶ Offers a wide range of products and services for residential and light commercial new construction and renovation properties. Whether you need a budget review, draw inspection, feasibility assessment or project review, we deliver superior customer service, technology innovations and industry leading turn times.

Trinity Loan Administration® LLC

▶ Delivers a comprehensive range of back office loan administration services, including builder reviews, collateral assessments, title reports, and lien waivers. Whatever the need, Trinity addresses and completes the administrative tasks of managing new construction or renovation loans, so customers can focus on their core business.

Trinity Residential Land Services® LLC

▶ Allows for coordination for residential property surveys. Trinity offers this service through a specially designed and easy-to-understand customer website. Check out: www.trinityrls.com

"A satisfied customer is the best business strategy of all."

~Michael LeBoeuf

Table of Contents

Introduction i

    Course Objectives i

    Course Overview ii

Module #1: 1

  The Fundamentals 1

    Pre-Closing 1

    Closing 1

    Post-Closing 1

Module #2: 3

  Construction Loans and Permanent Mortgages 3

    What is a Residential Construction Loan? 4

    Construction Loan Requirements 4

    Construction Loans vs. Mortgage Loans 6

    How does a Construction Loan Differ from a Permanent Mortgage? 6

    Interest Reserve 6

    Construction Funding 7

    Benefits of the Permanent Mortgage 8

    Secondary Market 8

    Two-Time Close versus One-Time Close 9

    Additional Revenue Opportunities for Construction Loans 10

    Summary 10

    Review 12

Module #3: 15

  Pre-Closing Phase 15

    Introduction to Pre-Closing Phase 15

    Builder Review 16

    Appraisals: The Valuation of a Property 17

    Understanding Appraisers 18

    Methods for Calculating Appraisals 19

    Collateral Review: Determining Project Feasibility 21

    Contract Review 22

    Types of Construction Contracts 22

    The Draw Schedule 23

    Collateral Assessment Report 23

    Title Review 27

Encumbrances 27

Title Examination 28

Title Insurance 28

Encroachments and Deed Restrictions 29

Bankruptcy Filings 30

Mechanic's Liens 30

Loan Processing 31

Credit Underwriting 31

Underwriters' Key Criteria 32

Denying a Loan 33

Review 34

Module #4: 37

Closing Phase 37

Introduction 37

Cash In and Out of Escrow 37

Down Payments and Borrower Equity 38

Documents, Closing and Final Settlement 39

Major Documents Required for Closing a Construction Loan 40

Review 43

Module #5: 45

Post-Closing Phase 45

Introduction 45

Initial Post-Close Meeting 46

Initial Draw 46

Draw Request Form 47

Permits 47

Builder's Risk Insurance 48

Survey and/or Foundation Endorsement 49

Mechanic's Lien Waivers 49

Mechanic's Lien Endorsement 50

Draw (Progress) Inspection 50

Architectural Approval 51

Subsequent Draws 52

Final Draw 52

Appraisal Update and/or Completion Report 53

Troubled Assets 53

    Loan Modification 57

    Conversion to Permanent Financing 60

    Review..62

Review Answer Key..63

Sample Reports and Forms...65

"Your customer doesn't care how much you know until they know how much you care."

~Damon Richards

Introduction

As an extremely cyclical industry, the real estate market remains ever-changing. In a few short years, the industry has soared to unexpected highs and plunged to unanticipated lows. Even while the United States housing market struggled to find equilibrium after the bubble burst and an intricate web of compliance regulations and laws were enacted, real estate remains a lucrative field, generating billions of dollars in revenue potential.

Real estate assets are continually bought, sold, developed, and re-developed. Though the real estate market is dynamic and developing, construction lending uses basic processes and guidelines. Trinity Real Estate Solutions wrote this book to serve as an instruction manual to this segment of the industry. Designed to work as a handbook, the information provides a basic understanding of residential construction lending, allowing readers to learn a wide variety of topics.

Construction lending techniques vary for each region of the United States. Because of these variations, not all aspects of residential construction lending can be covered. We suggest readers become familiar with additional information that may be pertinent to specific areas of the country and are region-defined.

It is our hope that this resource will provide general knowledge and familiarity, helping and assisting those navigating through the ever-choppy yet ever-fulfilling world of construction loans and financing.

Course Objectives

After completing this course, the participant will be able to complete the following:

► Explain a one-time close (OTC) loan and differentiate it from a two-time close.

► Analyze the three stages of a construction loan.

► Understand the relationship between the lender, builder and borrower.

► Define collateral review.

► Recognize the components of a first draw and understand the difference between a first draw and subsequent draws.

► Develop skills to deal with borrowers wanting to terminate a builder.

- ► Define a troubled asset and how it can harm lenders.

- ► Learn how to establish strong procedures during all phases of a residential construction loan.

Lesson Format

Each lesson follows the same format:

- Course Objectives

- Necessary Terms

- Lesson Content

- Review

Target Audience

This course is designed for anyone with an interest in the basics of residential construction lending and how it can be managed effectively for a lender and its associates.

Prerequisite Skills

None

Course Overview

This course contains five modules, which include objectives and review questions.

Module	Title
1	One Time Close Loans
2	Construction & Mortgage Loans
3	Pre-Closing
4	Closing
5	Post-Closing

Module #1:

The Fundamentals

Residential Construction Lending is not difficult, but it can be challenging. Many variables are involved in the process, including understanding the procedures, communicating them effectively, knowing your builder as well as other involved parties, and creating and distributing correct documentation.

The specifics within each loan vary but all lenders follow three phases in the construction lending process. These phases or steps include pre-closing, closing, and post-closing. To efficiently handle construction loans, lenders must recognize the differences between each stage.

Pre-Closing is the first phase of a construction loan. This phase involves the lender, borrower and builder, reviewing and approving all aspects of the transaction prior to commencement of construction. Credit reports, property appraisals, flood zone determination, builder reviews, title reviews, underwriting and other steps are completed, and ultimately, lenders reduce their risk by implementing strong policies and procedures throughout this phase.

Closing occurs after the loan is underwritten by the lender. A closing agent is engaged to finalize the loan and process various documents. During the loan closing process, all of the construction loan agreements are executed, and all instructions for processing the agreements and distributing funds are implemented.

Post-Closing is the last phase of the loan process. During this stage, construction begins and the borrower or builder requests "draws" or disbursements of construction funds. At this point in the process, loan officers, processors, underwriters and other loan origination personnel are no longer involved. Instead, the construction loan administration team supports and fulfills the lender's obligations under the loan agreement. The lender closely monitors the project to ensure the borrower is fulfilling commitments, including the agreement to build and protect the collateral from damage or deterioration.

Each phase is discussed in great detail within module 3, 4 and 5.

"Great things in business are never done by one person. They're done by a team of people."

~Steve Jobs

Module #2:

Construction Loans and Permanent Mortgages

Objectives

- ☐ Define a construction loan
- ☐ Describe a permanent mortgage
- ☐ Explain the differences between two-time and one-time close loans
- ☐ Understand the revenue potential for lenders

Necessary Terms to Understand the Following Modules

In the mortgage industry, professionals often speak in a unique language all their own, so this section begins with a cursory discussion about terms and definitions used throughout this module and within the industry as a whole:

- **Construction Loan**: A construction loan is a loan borrowed to finance the development of a home or another structure. It includes the costs of labor, materials, professional services, and administrative services during the building phase of a real estate project.

- **Mortgage Loan**: A mortgage loan is a written agreement for the temporary transfer of property (usually cash) used for the purchase or refinance of real estate opportunities, including homes, land, or commercial property. Within a mortgage loan, a lender receives the promise that the buyer will pay back funds within a certain time frame (e.g. five to 30 years) for a certain cost. A mortgage loan is legally binding and allows the lender the right to take legal claim against the borrower's property if he or she defaults on the terms of the note.

- **Two-Time Close Loan**: A two-time close loan is actually two separate loans. The first loan is executed on a short-term basis for the construction phase, and the second loan is a separate, permanent mortgage loan implemented on the completed project. The two-time close loan requires the homeowner to qualify for both loans independently, and the appeal of closing two loans separately lies in the flexibility of the lender selling the loan to investors. Typically, investor guidelines extend more grace towards a loan of a completed home than it does to a construction loan, and it's also advantageous to builders as it does not tie up the builder's credit line.

- **One-Time Close (OTC) Loan**: The one-time close loan is an extremely popular loan choice because it eliminates homeowners paying two sets of closing costs. Through this type of loan, closing costs are significantly reduced, and the homeowners may select their permanent interest rate during construction.

- **Escrow**: An escrow is a financial arrangement where a third party executes a list of instructions to close a real estate transaction. This agreement specifies how legal documents and money are to be collected, processed and redistributed to and from buyers and borrowers, sellers, lenders, realtors, and title companies.

- **Asset**: An asset is anything of value that can be converted into cash. Examples of assets include property, cash, real estate, machinery, and the right to receive repayment of a loan or intangibles, such as goodwill or intellectual property.

- **Collateral**: Collateral is property used as security for a loan in the event that repayment does not occur. A lender collects collateral to cover the payoff balance on a loan when borrowers fail to repay in full or protect and preserve the collateral property. Collateral applies to construction which has not been performed for both renovation or new construction. As a result, a lender's collateral review process for a construction loan is a bit more complex than a typical mortgage.

- **Lien**: A lien is a legal claim on someone's property and is used as security for debt. Liens may be both voluntary and involuntary in nature. Property owners typically consent to having voluntary liens placed on their property as a condition to obtaining a loan while an involuntary lien is a claim fixed against a property without the owner's agreement. Involuntary liens include local, state, and federal government tax liens or contractor or mechanics' liens, all used to encourage payment. Each state possesses specific guidelines to follow, which can impact the enforceability of the lien filed.

What is a Residential Construction Loan?

A residential construction loan is typically a short-term loan used to finance the building of a home or another real estate project. Generally underwritten for the length of time it takes to construct the home, this type of loan usually exists six to 36 months.

Construction Loan Requirements

Various documents are required for a construction loan, and each of these informational pieces are covered in subsequent chapters:

- Loan application
- Credit report
- Flood zone determination

- Appraisal
- Land survey
- Builder registration
- Title search and insurance
- Lien waivers
- Draw schedule
- Draw inspection request
- Draw inspection report

Most new construction loan documents establish dates for loan payoff, indicate deadlines to modify the loan into a permanent mortgage and determine when construction should be completed. These dates are modeled after the date of completion and documented within the construction contract. While the lender is not obligated to record these deadlines, hardships for both the borrower and builder will be avoided and alleviate the loan becoming a troubled asset for the lender down the road..

When creating the construction contract, it's imperative to begin with an accurate and complete set of construction plans and specifications. A common error occurs when homeowners remove items from their construction contract in an effort to cut costs, fully intending to pay for those items separately. Example items routinely left out of the construction contract include elements such as the well, septic, pool, or ancillary buildings. The easiest methodology to identify missing contract items is to meticulously review the contractor's line item cost breakdown and compare it with the appraisal or lender checklist. This process mitigates the risk of missing costs within the construction loan and provides increased security for the lender.

Construction loans also require the borrower, with the builder acting as the borrower's agent, to complete the construction as originally proposed. As with all mortgages, the borrower is required to demonstrate credit worthiness or the capability to repay the loan. The sale of individual homes in a subdivision or the procurement of some type of permanent financing are the most common methods for paying off a construction loan. Payoff methods vary, depending on the type of real estate the loan covers. Construction lenders must have an underwriting process in place prior to creation of a mortgage in order to reasonably protect the lender and ensure the borrower's ability to repay the construction loan. Additionally, after the construction loan is created, the lender must establish an efficient system to administer the construction loan and ensure loan funds are being used for the intended purposes of construction. Typically, the construction loan will follow a disbursement schedule, allowing the lender to exercise some control over the contractor and the construction.

The duration of the construction loan continues until completion of construction. In fact, within many municipalities, the finalization of construction concludes with the issuance of a Certificate of Occupancy by a city or county building and/or health departments. This document certifies a building's compliance, passing all required inspections and meeting health, safety and zoning or use requirements.

Construction Loans vs. Mortgage Loans

Lenders offer construction loans to finance both new or renovation real estate opportunities. Mortgage loans can be used to purchase an existing house or replace a current mortgage in order to provide the homeowner with more favorable loan terms, such as lower interest rates or longer repayment terms. Replacement of an existing mortgage is called "*refinancing*," and is utilized when a short-term construction loan replaces a longer-term "permanent" mortgage.

All mortgages are '*collateral*' loans because the lender takes a security interest in the real property. This security interest gives the lender the right to take possession of the property and sell it to repay the mortgage if the borrower fails to perform as discussed in the loan agreement. Failure to perform or pay back the loan as agreed upon in the terms of the mortgage is called a '*loan default*' and is defined as a breach in the loan documents. Examples of a default or breach might include (but are not limited to) failure to make timely payments due to construction inactivity, failure to build the house as originally proposed, failure to pay homeowners insurance and property taxes, failure to maintain the house in good condition and keep it free of other liens, or failure to complete construction prior to the agreed-upon maturity dates. Construction lenders must be aware of a possible breach or default and remedy the situation prior to funding the next construction draw. Funding a construction draw without correcting the breach/default could be interpreted as an 'implied approval' of the loan in its current stage and increases the inherent risk of the loan.

How does a Construction Loan Differ from a Permanent Mortgage?

A construction loan is defined as a short-term, interim loan when money is borrowed from a lender to pay for building of a new home. In contrast, a permanent mortgage loan, otherwise known as permanent financing, is obtained after completion of construction and is normally offered with a variety of rates and terms, ranging from 5 to 30 years, depending on the lender's menu of loan packages. Permanent mortgages cannot be used to pay for construction of a new home.

Construction loans are often compared to a giant credit card with collateral tied to it, sustaining only until the home is built. At completion, the borrower applies for or converts to a permanent mortgage for the finished house, and this permanent mortgage loan pays off the balance of the construction loan. Consequently, the primary difference between a construction loan and a permanent mortgage remains in the timing and direction of the flow of money between lender and borrower or the borrower's agent, the builder. With a construction loan, the lender advances funds to the borrower incrementally over time, called '*a draw*,' and these funds pay for the costs of construction as they become due. Each time the borrower requests funds, the lender generally inspects the property and verifies the completed work before funds are released.

Interest Reserve

During construction, a loan may include an interest reserve. An interest reserve is a special savings account funded out of the proceeds of a construction loan. In other words, the interest reserve is another line item in the cost breakdown of the construction loan, and essentially, it uses borrowed funds to pay interest on itself.

The minimum interest reserve is calculated as follows:

Committed Loan Amount X 70%[1] X Interest Rate / 12 X Construction Term

18 Month Example: $500,000 X 70% = $350,000 X 5.5% = $19,250
/ 12 = $1,604.17 (month) X 18 months = $28,875

Even though much variability exists in calculations between lenders and loan programs, the basic concept estimates the *average outstanding balance* during the construction phase and sets aside a sufficient portion of the loan amount to pay monthly interest on that balance.

One interesting note: interest reserves can mask risk issues within the construction loan. While the interest reserve may appear to be a performing loan, the homeowner may no longer be engaged. A lender may experience exposure if the loan is paying its own interest each month and at some point, the homeowner defaults on payments. In this case, the loan is only increasing, creating a loss at the end of its life cycle.

Construction Funding

In the absence of an interest reserve, borrowers must make interest payments to the lender out of their own funds. Disbursement of construction funds and/or interest payments by the lender causes the principal balance of the loan to increase. To a lender, a loan is an asset just as cash is an asset. When the borrower receives construction funds or draws from the interest reserve, the loan asset increases in size and value. At the same time, the lender depletes their own cash assets, so loan disbursements simply convert a cash asset into a loan asset. Removing one asset in order to increase another asset in and of itself does not increase the value for the lender. Likewise, from the borrower's perspective, receiving construction funds increases their debt while simultaneously boosting the value of their house as construction progresses. However, if managed correctly, both the borrower and the lender can benefit from the construction loan.

When the borrower pays interest on the construction loan, the lender recognizes a portion of the payments as income, increasing the lender's net worth. Of course, when the borrower completes the construction of the house, the structure should be worth more than the cost of construction, all due to careful planning and management of the development project. Wealth in the form of equity is created when the borrower completes a house that is worth more than the total cost of construction. Equity is simply the difference between the value of the property and the size of the lien or security interest the lender possesses in the property. An increase in equity produces an increase in the borrower's net worth. Because both the lender and the borrower take measurable risks to embark on a construction loan journey and building project, both deserve to be duly compensated for their efforts.

---

[1] This percentage is lender specific.

At this point, the borrower makes principal and interest payments to the lender each month until the principal balance is fully repaid. From the lender's perspective, principal payments reduce the loan asset by converting it to cash, and interest payments are compensation from the borrower for use of the lender's money. From the borrower's perspective, principal payments lower the cash outlet while also lessening debt, thus increasing the equity in the property.

Routinely, the principal balance of a construction loan is repaid in a lump sum at the completion of a project or by maturity of the lien. This occurs by selling the house, refinancing the construction loan to a permanent loan, or converting the loan from the construction phase to the permanent phase, also referred to as a one-time close. Two-time and one-time closes are discussed in greater detail later in this section. In either case, the permanent loan is immediately considered to be fully disbursed, and the lender has no further obligation to make advances to the borrower.

Benefits of the Permanent Mortgage

By replacing a construction loan with a permanent mortgage, both the borrower and lender benefit greatly. Generally, construction loans pose a higher risk for the lender than permanent mortgages because the collateral, which is a complete and habitable house, has yet to materialize. Any number of things can prevent the house from being completed. For instance, houses under construction are more vulnerable to weather and other natural disasters. Secondly, borrowers and builders may make mistakes or design changes during the construction process, causing the final project to be less valuable than the appraiser originally predicted. Furthermore, contractors can underestimate the cost of construction, resulting in an insufficient loan amount and an inability to cover the cost of completion. If cost overruns or shortages occur, mechanic liens could be the end result. Because of these additional risks, construction loans are generally more expensive to obtain than permanent mortgages for the borrower.

Secondary Market

Once construction is completed, the borrower may receive a lower interest rate when obtaining a permanent mortgage. While the lender assumes less risk, they benefit by selling the mortgage to institutional investors on the secondary mortgage market (discussed further in Module 5.) By pooling together large numbers of mortgages, selling bonds to investors, and repaying the bonds with the principal and interest payments collected from the group of borrowers, lenders can increase their value of the permanent mortgages.

In general, bond investors dislike risk incurred in construction loans, including the lack of certainty surrounding the completion of the house. Instead, investors desire predictable, timely cash flow with adequate security, which permanent mortgages provide. By selling permanent mortgages in the secondary market, lenders can charge investors monthly fees for monitoring borrower compliance with loan agreements and for collecting and distributing principal and interest payments. For most lenders, the monitoring of borrowers' compliance as well as collecting and redistributing borrower payments are performed by a business division separate from the origination of construction loans and permanent mortgages. Commonly called Loan Servicing or the Note Department, lenders can sell mortgage servicing rights (MSRs) to other lenders, who specialize in various funtions of servicing mortgages. Selling permanent mortgages and associated MSRs increases lender liquidity, allowing the creation of new mortgages to borrowers and subsequently, earn loan origination fees in the process.

Two-Time Close versus One-Time Close

As mentioned earlier, two types of construction loans are used when financing a new construction project: the one-time close and the two-time close loans.

Two-Time Close Loans

The two-time close construction loan is a traditional method for financing construction loans and consists of two parts: the initial short-term loan, which finances construction and the second long-term mortgage, which provides funding on the property once construction is complete. Two separate loans are used with two separate approval processes and closing periods.

Typically, the two-time close loan can be more expensive because it involves paying closing costs twice as the borrower acquires two separate loans. A two-time close also allows significantly more flexibility once construction is completed in regards to what permanent mortgage program will be selected. However, it does require the homeowner to be qualified twice.

In this scenario, the borrower pays for one appraisal for the construction loan and another appraisal for the permanent mortgage. During the time between construction and completion, changes in the borrower's credit profile or differences of opinion between two separate appraisers may occur, disqualifying the borrower or causing ineligibility for a permanent mortgage on the property. Understandably, these instances would cause concern since the lender could be relegated with a defaulted construction loan if the borrower is unable to pay the loan off upon completion of construction.

Two-time close loans present advantages to borrowers because they are not locked into a fixed loan amount and pay interest only on construction costs instead of the entire loan amount. In these cases, borrowers can receive lower interest rates on the second loan because their collateral is already in place.

One-Time Close Loans

The one-time close loan is a popular option for borrowers because it streamlines financing for construction of a home or other project. Also known as the construction-to-permanent loan, only one closing is required since the initial construction loan automatically converts to a long-term mortgage once construction is complete.

One-time close loans can be slightly less expensive and present less risk than a two-time close because they require only one loan. One-time close loans ask the borrower and lender to sign one set of loan documents and require only one set of closing fees, which is an attractive benefit for the borrower.

Additionally, the interest rate on a one-time close loan is established at inception. The rates and calculation methods (fixed, variable, interest only, fully amortizing, etc.) can be different during the construction phase versus the permanent phase, and the lender might even allow the borrower to choose from multiple interest rate options prior to converting from construction to permanent financing. As with the two-time close, if the borrower doesn't prefer the permanent mortgage options presented by the construction lender, he or she is free to shop elsewhere and refinance.

For these reasons, one-time close loans offer the borrower more flexibility and options than two-time close loans.

Additional Revenue Opportunities for Construction Loans

Not all lenders offer construction loans. Processing, underwriting and funding a construction loan requires many areas of expertise and pose additional risks not associated with purchase/refinance mortgages. Some construction lenders must assess whether a proposed construction project is viable, determine whether the construction loan and the borrower's contributed cash will be sufficient to complete the project, and judge whether the contractor is qualified to complete the job. Lenders who possess this expertise and effectively manage their risks can charge accordingly for their services. This specialized field of construction lending exposes lenders to new customers and opportunities since, in addition to the construction loan, these lenders often acquire the first and best opportunity to close the permanent mortgage. Regardless if the borrower keeps the new house or sells it to someone else, this area of mortgage lending can be very lucrative.

Summary

Purchasing a new home is one of the most rewarding and satisfying life experiences, yet many times it can also be a stressful venture. Construction loans and permanent mortgages are vital tools to ensuring the purchase occurs seamlessly. While both are critical components of the industry, each plays a specific role to ensure the process proceeds smoothly and without issues.

All loans, whether for new construction, existing home purchase or refinancing opportunities, are secured by the lender's right to seize the property partially or in full in the event the borrower fails to fulfill all of the requirements of the loan. Similarly, all mortgages can be repaid by either selling the mortgaged property or refinancing it. However, difficulties can develop when attempting to repay a construction loan if the construction has not been completed. Few homebuyers desire an uninhabitable home, and even fewer lenders will finance them. Permanent mortgages frequently have the added feature of allowing repayment up to 30 years by making monthly principal and interest payments. Construction loans differ from permanent mortgages in terms of (1) the loan purpose, (2) loan underwriting, (3) loan funding and (4) principal and interest repayment method.

As noted earlier, construction loans are intended as short-term financing to allow the time needed to construct a habitable home. When underwriting the borrower's ability for repayment of the loan as well as the adequacy of the collateral itself, the lender must consider the builder's ability to complete the construction. Otherwise, in the event of a loan default, the collateral is not likely to be sufficient to secure the loan. Whereas permanent mortgages are usually fully funded at inception followed by a long term principal and interest amortization schedule, construction loans are funded incrementally over the course of construction with only interest payment due from the borrower during construction. The construction loan might even permit the borrower to use loan funds to make interest payments and then add them to the principal balance.

Upon completion of construction, any loan can be repaid in full either by replacing it with a permanent mortgage or by selling the house. A two-time close construction loan requires the borrower to qualify for a new mortgage upon completion of construction. A one-time close construction loan adapts the construction loan to a permanent mortgage with only one set of closing costs. The remainder of the chapters will focus on the steps involved in originating the construction portion of the one-time or two-time close loan.

Once a construction loan is either converted to a permanent mortgage or refinanced by a permanent mortgage, the lender can deliver the new permanent mortgage to the secondary market to generate revenue and improve liquidity. Construction loans provide additional revenue generation opportunities that permanent mortgages do not. While serving a unique customer base typically with repeat business potential, construction lenders often charge more for their services due to the additional technical competencies required to succeed in this market.

Review

1. Define a construction loan:

_____

_____

_____

2. What are some of the similarities and differences between a construction loan and a permanent mortgage?

_____

_____

_____

_____

3. List the differences between two-time and one-time close construction loans.

_____

_____

_____

_____

4. Upon completion of construction, what are the borrower benefits when converting from a construction loan to a permanent mortgage? What are the benefits to the lender?

_____

_____

_____

_____

5. How do construction loans create additional revenue sources for lenders?

_____

_____

_____

_____

"You add value to people when you value them."

~John Maxwell

Module #3:

Pre-Closing Phase

Objectives

- ☐ Understand the different components of pre-closing
- ☐ Recognize how construction lending components interwork
- ☐ Prepare the loan for closing

Introduction to Pre-Closing Phase

Pre-Closing is the first phase of a construction loan. This phase plays a critical role in the process because it allows parties to review and approve all aspects of the transaction prior to the commencement of construction. Lenders navigate risk management well if they take control and establish strong policies within pre-closing.

Necessary Terms and Components to Understand Pre-Closing

- **Builder Review**: Consists of reviewing a builder's qualifications and determining qualifications to build the home in the location for the price offered.
- **Appraisal**: Assesses a property to determine the value of the loan collateral based on the loan closing date. The appraisal includes little, if any, improvements in place and is subject to completion of the construction. Lenders complete an appraisal in several ways, depending on the real estate in question.
- **Title Review**: Involves three different components:
  (1) The legal description of the property which serves as loan collateral,
  (2) The condition of the borrower's property title and the right to encumber it with a mortgage,
  (3) Pre-existing liens, which generally take priority over the lender's mortgage.
- **Loan Processing**: Collects all of the documents and necessary information to prepare the file for underwriting.
- **Underwriting**: Verifies the borrower's ability to repay the loan, the builder's qualifications to complete the construction and the suitability of the property to serve as collateral for the loan.
- **Draw Schedule**: Outlines a detailed payment plan for a construction project. Typically, the draw schedule determines when the lender disburses funds to the builder or the borrower for continuation of planned work.
- **Collateral Assessment Report**: Lists and evaluates specific securities and other property pledged by a borrower to secure repayment of a loan.

Builder Review: Determining the Best Fit

Within the construction loan process, one of the first and most significant decisions involves selecting a builder. Builder selection determines and controls how quickly and accurately construction will be completed, and typically, the borrower chooses his or her builder based on a number of factors. Lenders should not become involved in builder selection because it opens the door to potential liability for construction defects or other performance issues, which could lead to loan default.

From a selection process, builders must demonstrate a number of key factors to be considered, including a successful track record for completion of projects. Borrowers are encouraged to thoroughly evaluate the builder's prior client references and evaluate previous examples of work. While the lender holds the borrower responsible for their selection of a builder, the lender always reserves the right to reject a builder if he or she does not appear qualified to complete the project.

When selecting a builder, consider the following components:
1) Builder's payment history,
2) License history (if the project is situated in a jurisdiction that requires a license),
3) Quality and complexity of past projects and the similarity to the proposed construction under the loan,
4) History of litigation and consumer complaints,
5) Liability insurance and workman's compensation insurance (if required due to employees),
6) Financial capability to fund labor and material purchases between construction loan disbursements,
7) Years in business within the same market area,
8) Evidence of judgments, liens, bankruptcies, foreclosures all speak to a builder's ability to pay subs and suppliers timely,
9) Criminal Offenses.

During this procedure, lenders must consider the builder's criminal history. While a builder's ability to construct a home is not in question, the criminal history speaks to the character of a builder, and the need to do the right thing in difficult situations will arise routinely throughout construction.

Lenders are strongly recommended to never use words like "approve" or "qualify" in their loan documentation or in reference to a builder as these words may be interpreted as an endorsement or recommendation. Instead, lenders may inform borrowers of builder "acceptance" or "registration." Borrowers should understand that builder reviews are the lender's best opportunity to assess the risks of using a particular builder.

Appraisals: The Valuation of a Property

What is an Appraisal?

An appraisal is defined the act or process of developing an opinion for real property value.

When completing a construction project, the lender engages an appraiser to determine the economic feasibility of the subject property. By appraising the property, the lender determines if a subject property[2] adequately serves as collateral for a fully funded loan. Additionally, an appraisal decides if the value of the completed project will be equal to or greater than the cost of construction.

Within the appraisal process, a new construction appraisal answers the following questions:

1) 'What is the land worth?'
2) 'What will the structure be worth upon completion?'

In order to address these questions, the appraiser requests certain items including but not limited to:

1) Site plot plans
2) Building plans
3) Elevations[3]
4) Cost breakdowns
5) Material and fixture specifications
6) Descriptions of the mechanical systems[4] as well as other specialty features.

Armed with this information, the appraiser conducts a site inspection and researches recent listings and sales of comparable nearby properties ("comps" also called a "comparable") which refers to locations with characteristics that are similar to a subject's property. Ultimately, the appraiser's opinion of the completed project's value carries tremendous importance in the lender's decision to approve a construction loan. In the event the borrower does not repay the loan, the property becomes collateral which the lender can seize in an effort to be repaid.

---

[2] "Subject property" refers to the property that is the subject of the appraisal, i.e., the land, home or other item being appraised.
[3] Plans can include an overhead view of the site and the building itself as if the roof had been removed so one can see the placement of walls, doors, windows, etc. The plans show the size and location of the whole building as well as the individual rooms. Elevations are illustrations of the exterior walls and roof as they would appear to someone standing on the ground outside of the building.
[4] Mechanical systems typically include electrical systems, plumbing for fresh water delivery and sewage removal and heating, ventilation and cooling or "HVAC."

Property appraisal for construction loans are completed using the following:

- Building Plans: Construction drawings (also called plans, blueprints, or working drawings) are used to provide graphic and written information about a property for the actual building design.
- Specification Sheets: An explicit set of requirements that describes the exact materials to be used in the home's construction, including material, products and services.
- Cost Breakdowns: Systematic process of identifying the individual elements that comprise the total cost of dwelling construction. The cost breakdown assigns a specific dollar value to each element, and the value of the individual elements is expressed as a percentage of the total cost.
- Plot Plan: An architectural drawing that shows all of the major features and structures on a piece of property. Also known as site plans, these include the location of all buildings, porches, decks, landscaping features, and any other construction of an existing or proposed project site at a defined scale.

Understanding Appraisers

The real estate appraiser helps clients systematically determine an unbiased assessment and market value of a property, enabling the lender to make an informed lending decision. Appraisers are trained to not steer their opinion of value towards a figure that is expected or suggested by their client. Instead, their opinions are guided entirely by objective and verifiable market data. Appraisers should not have a personal relationship of any sort with their client(s), the lenders, buyers or sellers of the subject property as this may create the appearance of influence over their professional opinion and the appraisal outcome.

Appraisers are licensed according to the rules of the individual states in which they operate. Each state dictates detailed processes and minimum qualifications to perform as a licensed appraiser. In addition to being certified by the state, an appraiser must be knowledgeable about the property type and the specific neighborhood in which the property is located. In some instances, lenders retain appraisers directly on their staff, who appraise the properties themselves; however, more commonly, lenders select and approve an Appraisal Management Company (AMC) to fulfill real estate appraisal assignments on their behalf. Using an extensive network of independent appraisers located in broad geographic areas, the AMC reviews and approves appraisers' qualifications and the quality of their work. Lenders may also use an in-house appraiser to conduct secondary reviews of the appraisal reports for accuracy, demonstrating the importance lenders place on the quality of appraisal reports. All lenders must establish a system to assure only qualified appraisers receive their appraisal requests, and the final appraisal reports are completed accurately and meticulously.

With more than 82,000 active real estate appraisers in the U.S. the Appraisal Institute is the nation's largest trade organization for appraisers. Organized in 1932, the Appraisal Institute 'advances professionalism and ethics as well as global standards, methodologies and practices through the professional development of property economics.' The majority of Appraisal Institute professionals are practicing real estate appraisers and property analysts, providing valuation-related services to clients such as mortgage lenders, financial institutions, government agencies, attorneys as well as homeowners, and other individual consumers. The organization provides various designations to some of its members, depending on the types of appraisal services, the types of properties and their specific level of expertise the individuals possess.

Currently the Appraisal Institute offers a few key membership designations:
- Member Appraisal Institute (MAI) designation: Earned by appraisers with experience in the valuation and evaluation of commercial, industrial, residential and other types of properties. The MAI designation is widely recognized as the most prestigious achievement an appraiser can achieve.
- Senior Residential Appraiser (SRA) designation: Held by professionals who provide a wide range of services in the analysis and valuation relating to residential properties.

Both of these designations indicate an appraiser is qualified to review the work of other appraisers. To become more familiar with the various professional designations or to locate appraisal professionals, visit the Appraisal Institute's web site at http://www.appraisalinstitute.org.

Methods for Calculating Appraisals

For construction loans, appraisers generally use two approaches to value in Appraisal Practice when determining the Market Value of a new property.

Cost Approach

The first approach for determining market value is the *cost approach,* which assumes a potential user of real estate wouldn't or shouldn't pay more for a property than it costs to build an equivalent structure.

With the cost approach methodology:
market price for a property = the cost of land + cost of construction less depreciation.

The cost approach is especially useful for unique properties without good comparable examples. This model is more valuable for estimating the value of newer properties since current construction costs are often well known.

Because the value of the lot is critical to mitigating the risk of overpaying for the lot, the appraiser's opinion of site value is relied upon within the cost approach to ensure over funding doesn't occur. Often front-loaded contracts include the lot and construction, which may over-value the lot. This is generally not an issue for the lender unless a builder abandons the project before or during construction.

Additionally, lenders may encounter an appraiser who measures the value of the completed home but does not put much effort into the value of the land. Most of the comparable properties in the appraisal will be completed structures. Thus, it is critical to require a valid lot comparable to support the opinion of site value.

In general, appraisers are not contractors. If there is a large disparity between the appraiser's construction cost estimate and the borrower's construction budget, lenders should take notice. If the appraiser has under-estimated or over-estimated the cost of construction, the borrower may be undercharged or overcharged by the contractor, which leads to potential problems during construction. While being undercharged doesn't sound like a problem at first, an underestimated budget foretells potential problems such as available construction funds (the combination of borrower supplied funds and lender supplied funds) being depleted before construction is complete. As discussed in module 5, a major cause of non-performance on construction projects is created by an underestimation of the budget. If the contractor overcharges the borrower, he or she should request to revisit the calculations with the contractor or investigate hiring a new one.

Sales Comparison Approach

A second approach used to value a residential property is the *sales comparison approach*. The sales comparison approach compares recently-sold properties to an original subject property in a similar marketplace. Price adjustments are made for differences in the comparable and subject properties, considering market place conditions and the properties characteristics of value.

For example, an appraiser using the sales comparison approach for a residential property would locate an identical property with an exception that it has one additional bathroom and a smaller lot size. The appraiser then applies a negative adjustment for the additional bathroom and a positive adjustment to the smaller lot size in order to arrive at the theoretical price the buyer would theoretically pay.

When evaluating appraisers' work, lenders should closely scrutinize the choice of comps and question large adjustments, which are indicative of non-comparability. Sale comparables sold in the distant past or located in dissimilar neighborhoods with external factors should be avoided. These external factors might include the availability of utilities, the quality of schools, maintenance of public streets and parks or noxious influences, such as traffic or heavy industry. Sometimes, a property located just a few blocks away but on the other side of a busy freeway could carry a huge difference in value than the subject property.

In many cases, an appraiser will use both approaches to determine the appraised value of a property. If the values from both calculations do not support one another, the proposed construction may be "overbuilding the area" within the local market, resulting in an inflated loan amount compared to the appraised value. Overall, an appraiser must possess an abundance of experience in new construction to complete an appraisal, including the expertise to read and understand construction plans, interpret specifications, and evaluate structures that don't yet exist. Likewise, construction lenders must understand the correct questions to ask and recognize if the 'subject to completion' appraisal is accurate.

Two questions to ask:

1) Does the subdivision or the area have the necessary infrastructure (roads, electric, water, sewer) to support construction?

2) Is the value of the home contingent on the subdivision amenities? Subdivision amenities vary in value, and amenities such as golf courses and equestrian centers can add significant value to the homes in a neighborhood, but only if those amenities are complete. Conversely, the value of a subdivision will decrease significantly if the developer did not plan for or depleted funding before completing the amenity packages. The appraiser fully understands the current status of the community amenities and how it affects the lot value as well as the 'as completed' value.

In the glossary of this book, please find an example of an appraisal report typically used for a new construction project. The report has a section for the appraiser to use and apply each of the methods discussed in this module.

Collateral Review: Determining Project Feasibility

As discussed previously, collateral is defined as property used to secure a loan. If a loan is not repaid, the lender generally confiscates the collateral through a foreclosure process and sells it to repay the loan. In the case of new construction, the collateral value may be limited to the value of the land on the day the loan is originated.

Cautious construction lenders ensure the following:

1) All costs are accounted for in a thorough and accurate budget.
2) The combination of borrower and lender funds is sufficient to cover all costs.
3) Any overall construction cost deficiencies are identified and addressed.
4) The proposed home can be placed in the subdivision as proposed in difference to any developer restrictive covenants.
5) The home appraised is also supported by the construction documents (contract, plans, specs, cost breakdown).

Collateral review may occur concurrently with the underwriter's review of the borrower's information and the appraisal. Lenders use collateral reviews to protect themselves from risks that arise from budget deficiencies and under-qualified contractors. The reviewer then reconciles the appraisal with the construction contract to ensure they cover the same features and envision the same completed improvements. Reviewers search for items in the contract not included in the appraisal and vice versa. The outcome of the review informs the lender if he or she can reasonably expect the project to be completed for the amount budgeted while attaining the expected value estimated by the appraiser. Reviewers must possess the expertise needed to review building plans, construction budgets, title reports and appraisal reports. After compiling and reviewing all of the data, the reviewer will summarize their findings in the collateral assessment report.

Contract Review

The construction contract is an integral part of the mortgage framework and the appraisal. The contract typically exists between a home buyer and the builder. Many types of construction contracts exist but all should contain several essential elements:

- What is being offered?
  - The construction of a home
- What is the consideration for the offer?
  - o The cost for the home
- How will the consideration be paid?
  - o Draw schedule
- How long will construction take?
  - o What's the remedy if the timeframe is not met?
- Where will the construction take place?
  - o The address
- What parties are included in the contract?
  - o Homebuyer and Builder
- How will change order be handled?
  - o Documented plus inform the lender

Lenders beware -- missing just one element from a contract after the loan closes can be problematic.

Types of Construction Contracts

Numerous types of construction contracts can be used within a construction project, but within this text, the three most common are covered.

A **cost plus contract** charges the homebuyer the cost of the invoices 'plus' a percentage to the builder. Builders favor these contracts because they are not tied to a final price. Homebuyers appreciate this type of contract as they are only tied to the actual cost (plus a percentage). However, lenders should not accept this type of construction contract without a specified contingency arrangement, ensuring any cost overages are built into the construction budget or the homebuyer and the builder provide a 'maximum cost' for construction.

A **management contract** is primarily used for the contractor that is functioning as a project coordinator. In this case, the contract appoints the homeowner as the party responsible for issuing the project's payments. The coordinator's fee is a fixed dollar amount but doesn't include the construction costs, and payments are based on completed phases of construction or on a specified amount of time. If delays occur within construction, the coordinator's fee may be fully paid out prior to completion of the home, potentially causing his or her attention to wane and increasing lender risk. Typically, a fixed price is not associated with a management contact. If a maximum cost exists within the management contract, a section for cost over-runs and the one responsible for payment will be specified. If the homeowner is responsible, the cost truly isn't 'fixed.' It is recommended that lenders not accept this type of construction contract without a specified contingency built into the construction budget for cost overages.

From the lender's perspective, a **fixed price contract** is the optimum contract for new construction financing because it offers stability and a predictable scenario for both parties during the contract length. A fixed price contract sets an established price for the construction of the home, and a section within this contract addresses the responsible party for cost over runs. If the homeowner is responsible for overages, this contract changes from a 'fixed price' to a "cost plus" contract. A fixed price contract promises to deliver the completed home for the set price, easing the burden of financing the home.

While no contractual obligations exist between a builder and the lender, a fiduciary trust may be required for the project to run smoothly. A contract structure must be created between lender and borrower and between builder and borrower. While the lender and builder function in acknowledgement of the other's contract, they are not actually engaged or obligated to one another. However, throughout the construction loan, lenders must complete this critical step and confirm a builder's funding expectation is in line with the lender's funding practice. If the terms of the construction contract cannot be honored by the lender, notifying the builder in advance will encourage communication and mitigate risk in the long run. Ultimately, wise lenders compare a construction contract to their loan documents, reviewing discrepancies, recognizing maturity dates and funding practices, and identifying costs that may be missing from the project.

The Draw Schedule

Disputes surrounding the draw schedule are very common between builders and lenders. Typically, lenders only fund work that is completed and in place. If the construction contract calls for deposits or funding for materials on site, issues may occur for the builder when items or deposits aren't funded during construction. The draw schedule, whether it is in the construction contract or within the loan documents, should be agreed upon by all parties prior to closing.

Collateral Assessment Report

The Collateral Assessment report is a critical document that provides evaluation of collateral risks, allowing an underwriter to assess loan viability. The report itself begins with 'Header' data, which outlines the lender, borrower and builder contact information. It also includes a high level summary of the project and a sketch of the project's front elevation for quick graphic identification.

The next two sections, the 'Notice of Findings' and the 'Outstanding Builder Conditions/Recommendations,' alert the lender to any material findings or areas of concern. These sections provide recommended steps to alleviate any concerns surrounding the builder's credentials or other key elements. A collateral review should include a builder review as it will either strengthen or weaken the project recommendation.

The report further discusses detailed descriptions of the reviewer's findings, including cost variances between the line item cost breakdown from the borrower and the respective contractor to the lender. The information documents the appraiser's cost approach, variances between how much the borrower is paid (or is paying) for the site value used in the appraiser's cost approach, settlement of the lot purchase, and the accuracy of the construction loan budget. Reports may vary regarding the amount of information because of the lender information, appraisal information and the construction contract itself.

A review section is followed by a checklist, which further explains specific comments and allows the reviewer to individually respond to line summaries corresponding to comments. The checklist allows the lender to better understand what contributed to the reviewer's opinion about items that require additional attention.

On the following two pages, a sample collateral assessment report is attached, demonstrating a typical report produced by Trinity Loan Administration.

TRINITY
Loan Administration, LLC

Collateral Assessment

Report Date:	**04-30-2014**	**Borrower Name:**	**Pierce and Charlotte Smith**
Loan #	**042819679527**	**Borrower Phone #:**	**972-865-0257**
Lender:	**Trinity Loan Bank**	**Borrower Email:**	**p&csmith@gmail.com**
Lender Contact:	**Jerry Sattler**	**Builder Name:**	**Levi Construction LLC**
Lender Contact #:	**972-865-0257**	**Builder Contact :**	**Levi Scruggs**
Lender Email:	jerry.sattler@trinityonline.com	**Builder Email**	**levi@leviconstructionllc.com**
Trinity Order #:	**13-528774**	**Construction Type**	**Single Family**
Product Type	**One Time Close**	**Disposition:**	**Approved W/Conditions**

Address: 750 Fairlway Drive, Wylie TX 75098

FRONT ELEVATION

Collateral Summary:

Subject is a proposed 3,303 sf Detached Traditional style Single Family Home on an improved 14,084sf site and is typical for the market being built in.

The property is located within an established development.

The construction contract is a fixed price agreement.

There is a minimum variance (-4%) between appraiser's cost approach and the construction contract.

The appraisal has multiple comparables for the lot which supports the builder's lot cost noted.

Notice of Findings

- Please provide evidence of the initial deposit amount ($84,505.66) has been received by the builder. (Cancel check or a signed receipt from the builder)

- Please provide a copy of the title commitment and subdivision's restrictive covenants.

- Please provide a construction loan budget that splits the lot value of $60,000 and the construction costs of $362,528.29 and does not have any negative numbers.

Contingency requirements are waived for Levi Construction LLC. See Builder Assessment

Outstanding Builder Conditions / Recommendations

- Builder's License No.04281967 expires 10/31/2014 and will require evidence of renewal

Reserves/Direct Cost Analysis	N/A	Yes	N
Is the Builder registered and all project related conditions met on the Builder Review?			
Is the builder registration in the correct geographic location without conditions or limitations?			
Is the variance between the appraised value and the contracts less than 20%?			
Contracts	N/A	Yes	N
Is the construction contract total amount the same as Direct Costs on the budget?			
Are all construction costs covered within the construction contract and noted on the Construction Loan Budget? (well, septic, pool, & by owner items)			
Is the construction term sufficient for the size & location of the project and in agreement with the contract and policy?			
Is the construction contract fully executed?			
Does construction contract comply with Lenders disbursement guidelines?			
Have the Building Plans been submitted to the local municipality for approval?			
Is the cost of the modular, log or kit home shown separately from construction costs?			
Is there a detailed cost breakdown for all site work?			
Does the construction loan budget reflect a minimum contingency of 5% of the direct costs?			
Rehabs	N/A	Yes	N
Does Land/Existing Improvements on the budget equal appraised market value minus direct costs (if seasoned)? (Purchase price prevails if not seasoned.)			
Does the construction loan budget reflect a minimum 10% contingency as required for rehab projects?			
Line Item (Required on Rehabs; Cost-Plus; and Consultant)	N/A	Yes	N
Does the line item cost breakdown add up correctly (run tape)?			
Does Line Item Cost Breakdown match the Contract amount?			
Does Line Item Cost Breakdown reflect the costs for all major components and finish items (flooring, countertops, cabinets, landscaping, etc.) to complete the project?			
Construction Loan Budget	N/A	Yes	N
If this is a modular or log kit project, is the contract amount on the "Modular/Kit/Log" line and the site work on the "Direct Costs" line?			
Have all deposits towards construction been verified?			
Is the initial draw at closing (including direct & indirect costs) equal to or less than 10% of the direct costs?			
Have all indirect costs being paid at closing been documented sufficiently?			
Is the property address noted correctly on all corresponding documentation (construction contract, appraisal, title commitment, lot contract (if applicable), and construction loan budget)?			
Is the Construction Loan Budget free of any negative totals?			
Land Value	N/A	Yes	N
If Land is being purchased as part of this transaction, is the land amount on the budget the same as the contract amount?			
Is there evidence of the lot purchase?			
Is the land value on the construction loan budget greater than the appraised land value?			
Appraisal	N/A	Yes	N
Does the appraiser indicate the improvements are "proposed"? (If Rehab, "existing" is acceptable.)			
Does the appraiser indicate the rights are "fee simple"?			
Does the appraisal include photos of the building site (front and street scene) and comps?			
Has construction started?			
Do appraisal photos show an existing manufactured home?			
If there is an existing structure located on the site, has the cost for the removal been documented and placed on the Construction Loan Budget? (Unless subject project is a Rehab)			
If work has started (or Rehab) has proof of builder's risk / course of construction insurance been provided?			
Does Appraiser comment on infrastructure?			
Does Appraiser support the lot value with lot comps?			

Title Review

"Title" is a legal method, asserting an individual owns partial or full rights or ownership to a property. As customary with most real estate transactions, verification of title begins once the appraiser completes the appraisal report. Conceptually, rights in real property are far ranging and must be spelled out in meticulous detail.

Following is a brief list of property rights examples:

- The right to occupy a property for a limited time (leasehold interest)
- The right to extract underground minerals without touching the surface (mineral rights)
- The right to travel across the surface without permanently occupying the property (access easement)
- The right to bury utilities (gas, electric, cable) beneath the property and periodically maintain it (utility easement)
- The right to permanently occupy, build upon, raise crops, extract water and minerals and sell to a new owner in due course (fee interest)
- The right to prevent a subsequent owner from operating a business on the property or limiting the types of structures that can be placed upon it (deed restriction)
- An owner's right to be in title to anything below the surface of the land without disturbing anything above the surface of the land, i.e. oil or mineral rights
- The right to collect property taxes, homeowner's association dues, or other debts from the owner, such as an unpaid mortgage, including by a forced sale of the property if necessary (liens)

Encumbrances

Mortgages and other liens on title are labeled 'encumbrances' because they restrict the owner's ability to transfer title to a property or lessen its value until the claim is lifted. Encumbrances include liens, deed restrictions, easements, encroachments and licenses.

Title is conveyed to a new owner or modified by the existing owner by drafting and recording[5] a deed within the county public records where the property is located. Likewise, liens can be recorded against a property if the lienholder believes he or she has a valid claim. If the property owner consents to a lien, such as a mortgage, the lien is voluntary. Involuntary liens include property taxes or a judgment lien and occur when the property owner is not required to give consent for the lien to be enforceable. When title passes from one owner to another, all rights assigned to the property remain on title unless they are modified by the person or entity owning the right to modify it. If an owner's or other lienholder's bundle of rights or title is unclear, the ability to assert those rights may be

---

[5] By recording documents, they become public records that anyone can access. Granted, it might take some expertise to know how to locate a particular record through County Recorder's office. Attorneys, title companies, appraisers, realtors and many others possess this expertise. Even if a layperson lacks this expertise, by the document having been recorded, you are deemed by the law to have been constructively notified of it. Much of the information in a title policy is retrieved from the County Recorder's public records.

impaired. Easements and deed restrictions are common forms of impairment, and their effects on the rights of ownership are measurable, predictable and perfectly acceptable to a lender. However, lack of clarity or uncertainty arising from poorly defined rights can create difficulty when assigning value to property or assessing the risks of ownership for a lender.

Title Examination

Title examination is crucial in a real estate transaction as it assures a borrower or lender that no other interest exists on a real estate property. Real estate lenders are prospective owners of collateral property, so they assert the right to assume the borrower's property title in the event of a loan default. Lenders must compare the original property to the condition of a borrower's title to learn of any issues that might impair their right of ownership, the eventual sale of a property or the potential repaying of a loan. "Clouds" on title refer to concerns or issues that might invalidate or impair an owner's intended use of the property. If clouds are discovered on a title when underwriting a loan, the borrower must take corrective legal action to clear the cloud or the loan will be declined outright.

The rights of lienholders or those who hold an interest in an item of property are granted certain rights to a property based on the chronological order of the recording date. For example, if party A sues a property owner for the collection of a debt and wins the lawsuit, party A can record a lien against the property in the amount of the judgment. Later, if party B grants a construction loan to the property owner and records a mortgage against the property, party A's judgment lien takes priority over party B's mortgage. In other words, when the property is sold, party A's judgment lien must be satisfied in full before any of the sale proceeds may be applied to party B's mortgage. Both party A and party B are repaid in full before the owner can receive any sale proceeds.

Title Insurance

Lenders may examine the condition of title to property by obtaining a title insurance policy. A real estate purchaser must protect against serious financial loss due to a possible defect in the property purchase. Before a mortgage is granted, the lender obtains a preliminary title policy from the title insurer, which shows the condition of title. If the lender accepts the condition of title, grants the mortgage, and pays the title insurance premium to the insurer, the insurance policy goes into effect, and the cost of the policy is usually charged to the borrower. The title insurance policy names the legal owner(s) of the property, provides a physical legal description[6] of the property and lists all of the registered liens, mortgages,

---

[6] Legal descriptions usually take the form of a (1) metes-and-bounds survey, (2) lot and tract number or (3) sectional survey. Metes-and-bounds surveys name a beginning point such as a permanent monument, street intersection or geographic feature and proceed to describe the length and compass orientation of each boundary line of the property in succession. Thus, if one were to walk the lines in the order described, they would return to the point of beginning. Lot and tract numbers refer to individual lots that are part of a subdivision plat recorded in the public records. Sectional surveys describe land as being portions of townships. Townships are six mile by six mile tracts of land divided into 36 one mile square sections. Each section contains 640 acres. Any portion of a section can be described by fractionally dividing the section (e.g. "the southern half of the western half of the northeast quarter of section 12) until only the subject property remains. Throughout much, but not all, of the Unites Statesman series of intersecting north/south meridians and east/west baselines exist, and each intersection has a unique name. Townships are arranged

easements, etc. Various recordings against the property are called "exceptions from coverage," and in these cases, the title policy does not insure the lender against the priority of these recordings over the lender's mortgage. Essentially, the title policy ensures the owner identity, the legal description and the coverage exceptions are accurate. If this information is incorrect and the insured lender is damaged as a result of the inaccuracy, the title insurer will defend against any damage. Payment of a prior lien or hiring an attorney may be executed to defend the insured property's title in a Court of Law.

When lenders review a preliminary title insurance policy, a primary concern exists to review the owner's equity in the property, which is the value of their ownership interest after all existing liens have been satisfied. Specifically, lenders must ensure the policy will be sufficient to repay the mortgage. Nearly all property has a yearly property tax lien filed against it, which takes priority over all other liens. Lenders will insist that the taxes are paid current, so in no uncertain terms, any liens for past due taxes are unacceptable in the lenders' eyes.

Encroachments and Deed Restrictions

Lenders are also accustomed to seeing easements on properties for items such as utilities and public roadways, as long as the footprint of the proposed construction does not sit on top of, or "encroach" upon, the easement. Municipalities frequently place limits on the locations of buildings within a parcel of land, and structures must be positioned a minimum distance from the front, rear and sides of the parcel. Setbacks do not typically appear on a title report, and the municipality granting the building permits must verify compliance with setback requirements. If lenders are concerned about the risk of encroachment on easements, setbacks or the property boundary, they regularly purchase insurance in the form of a foundation endorsement from the title company.

Lender's objectionable exceptions from coverage typically include deed restrictions, additional property owners (other than the loan applicant), prior mortgages[7], judgment liens and mechanic's liens. If a deed restriction does not allow usage on the property that is the objective of the construction loan, i.e. to erect a building on the property, the restriction will be required to be removed[8] before the loan transaction can be closed. Naturally, lenders expect all property owners to consent to the placement of a new mortgage by requesting their signature on the mortgage agreement. If a borrower owns a prior mortgage on title, and they default on that mortgage, a foreclosure from the prior lender occurs and that lender takes ownership of the property. In this case their foreclosure would generally extinguish, or render useless, the lien rights of the subsequent mortgagee.

---

like a patchwork quilt relative to these intersections. They are numbered according to their range east or west of the intersection and their township north or south of the interest ("… of township 3 south, range 5 east, San Bernardino Base and Meridian.")

[7] If the lender is deliberately granting a junior (e.g. "second") mortgage, he or she will typically stipulate that a default on the senior mortgage constitutes a default on the junior mortgage. In the event of a default on the senior mortgage, the junior mortgagee holds the right to cure the default on the senior mortgage and recover the cost thereof from their borrower.

[8] Removal can be accomplished in a variety of ways. The party who places the restriction might be willing to remove it by recording a document called a deed rescission. The property owner might also be able to force a rescission via legal action and Court order.

Of course, it is not uncommon for a lender to use a portion of their mortgage to pay off or refinance an existing mortgage in order to clear it from title. Some judgment liens and mechanic's liens can be effectively foreclosed upon through a court ordered sale of the property, which could conceivably have the same consequence as the foreclosure of a prior mortgage. Liens also include the lienholder's right to recover legal fees and costs of collection, which increases the difficulty in quantifying the lienholder's potential interest in the property. Sometimes these exceptions are due to oversights by the title company or the misfiling of paperwork with the court. In these cases, the lender can usually work through the title company to correct the error and proceed with the mortgage transaction. However, if the exceptions are legitimate, the lender will require the borrower to clear them before proceeding, often by paying off the lien. Lienholders are encouraged to subordinate their claims to the new mortgage, which lowers the priority of a claim under a new mortgage. In exchange for subordination, lienholders may demand some form of compensation from the property owner.

Bankruptcy Filings

Bankruptcy filings often appear as an additional item on preliminary title reports, and if correct, they prevent a mortgage transaction from closing. *Bankruptcy* is a legal proceeding provided under federal law, allowing an individual or corporation to halt the collection efforts of creditors while attempting to reorganize or discharge certain obligations. Title companies, in addition to credit bureaus, usually check the U.S. Bankruptcy Court records to understand if a property owner has a bankruptcy case pending. In general, bankruptcy filings reflect poorly on the borrower's credit quality and impact the ownership interest in the property. In this case, the property owner holds no right to encumber the property with additional debt, and if the lender were to proceed with granting a new mortgage, it could be unenforceable.

Mechanic's Liens

A mechanic's lien is a security interest within the property's title for the benefit of those who have supplied labor or materials to improve a property. Despite its name, mechanic's liens are typically used by subcontractors and suppliers and are a legal claim against a property that has been remodeled or improved. Mechanic's liens can occur when a supplier or subcontractor is not compensated for work completed.

Often, mechanic's liens do not appear on a preliminary title report, and their rights vary from state to state. In many regions, the priority of mechanic's lienholders' rights date back to the time when they first provided labor or materials, even if they have not yet filed a lien. A condition called 'broken priority' exists when work has already begun on the construction project, and the mechanic's lien was filed after the new mortgage was recorded. In this case, broken priority takes precedence over the mortgage just as if it actually appeared in the coverage exceptions on the preliminary title report. For this reason, lenders are always advised to visually inspect the site of the proposed construction before closing the loan. If as much as a construction fence or portable sanitary facility was delivered to a site, many lenders will refuse to proceed with a construction loan. In this case, the developer is required to delay the closing of the loan until the statutory period for the filing of mechanic's lien has expired.

Loan Processing

Once title is reviewed and all of the liens are determined, the loan processing step occurs. Within this stage, the processor prepares the loan information and application for the underwriter to review. In short, processing is the collection of a myriad of documents the underwriter needs in order to render a credit decision. A loan officer reviews the initial application, orders a credit report on the borrower and sends an initial list of documents needed for the processor. The loan officer will also forward the application, the credit report and any other received documentation from the borrower to the processor.

To anticipate which records will be required from the borrower, processors must be extremely familiar with underwriting requirements. Usually, this information includes a large amount of documentation, including the borrower's credit quality, employment, income, expenses, liquid assets, source of down payment and other obligations. The processor will also verify much of this documentation independently. Employers must be confirmed and additional information will be collected on the proposed mortgaged property, including the appraisal, construction plans, line item cost breakdown, construction contract, building permits and builder credentials (license, insurance, experience, etc.). If the processor produces a complete and orderly loan file, a great deal of time can be saved in underwriting, and the loan transaction can quickly proceed.

Credit Underwriting

Once loan processing is complete, the loan proceeds to underwriting, which can be one of the more obscure parts of the lending process. Generally, borrowers understand a great deal about the application stage because they are actively involved in it. Likewise, they are aware of what takes place at closing because they are present for the process. But it is this middle stage, known as underwriting, that raises many questions amongst home buyers.

Underwriting is the process where a lender quantifies risk and verifies compliance of the transaction within their loan program requirements. Underwriting requires experience, sound judgment and a detailed understanding of loan program requirements. The lender establishes these requirements if they intend to hold the loan on their books and bear all risk of repayment. However, if the loan is intended to be sold in the secondary market or insured by a government agency or private mortgage company, the investor may have extensive underwriting criteria of their own. In either case, failure to meet specific and detailed program requirements can result in the lender being unable to sell or insure the loan, which downgrades the quality of the asset.

The underwriter examines every aspect and qualification of the borrower, the property and the builder eligibility for the loan program in question. Underwriters also question the legitimacy of the documentation provided, the accuracy of the appraisal, and the veracity of the borrower's income and asset documentation. They inquire about the plausibility of the borrower's stated intentions for the mortgaged property or the ability of the builder to competently complete the construction. Ultimately, an underwriter will ensure the borrower's financial profile matches the lender's guidelines and loan criteria before moving forward with the loan.

Underwriters' Key Criteria

Underwriters are trained to look for items that give rise to suspicion. With that purpose, what does an underwriter look for when reviewing a loan? In a word -- *everything*. An underwriter's overall goal is to confirm and insure the loan and question whether the borrower intends to occupy a location as their primary residence.

For example, if a borrower with a large family is building a small home, does it make sense that they would move their large family into the small home? Or could the borrower be speculating to build the home for immediate sale and profit? If a home is built in an out-of-state resort area located far from the place of employment, could the home be used as a second or vacation home? Additionally, are two payments needed and affordable? Underwriters investigate every aspect of the borrower's documents to ensure all of the information is complete, valid, and reasonable.

An underwriter will conduct an in-depth analysis of the borrower's ability to repay the loan with a focus on income and asset documentation, employment history, credit history and the borrower's current credit profile. Obtained from the credit report, the borrower's credit score remains an important level indicator of their history of meeting obligations, and a high credit score indicates a reduced credit risk for lenders. The credit report also provides details on the amount borrowed and the repayment history for existing money owed as well as debt that has been fully repaid or charged by other creditors. Because lenders are especially sensitive to the borrower's history of repaying mortgage debt, a past default on a mortgage could disqualify a borrower for a new mortgage regardless of their credit score.

A complete income analysis is conducted in order to determine the borrower's capacity to make the payments on the requested mortgage. Through this process, the underwriter considers employment, income, assets and any other obligations the borrower is repaying. The capacity to service debt is measured by a debt-to-income ratio, calculating the sum of all monthly loan payments the borrower will be making divided by the sum of all income being received. The rules for calculations are spelled out in detail in the loan program guidelines, which will specify some threshold the ratio must not exceed.

Additionally, the stability of one's employment also factors into loan eligibility. An individual's current source of income as well as the type of income generated is carefully considered. When reviewing employment, an underwriter might question the likelihood of a person earning hourly wages and their probability to maintain the same hours per week. If the borrower is self-employed or earning a commission, the underwriter may challenge how much experience the borrower possesses and how successful he or she may be under various future economic scenarios. Salaried employees are considered to have the most stable income since their hours do not typically vary.

Some loan programs require escrow for property taxes, homeowners' insurance and/or payment of mortgage insurance premiums. In these cases, the underwriter will prepare an escrow worksheet, calculating the precise amount to collect from the borrower at the loan closing. The monthly amount going forward along with the monthly mortgage payment will be assessed, ensuring that funds for taxes and insurance will be available when they come due. The escrow provides protection and convenience for all parties involved because it assures the borrower is setting aside funds each month for payment, and it permits the lender to control the timely disbursements for tax authorities and insurers.

Underwriters also consider and evaluate contractor's qualifications. In addition to verifying their appropriate licenses, liability insurance and workmen's compensation insurance for their employees, the underwriter reviews items such as number of homes built per year, size and costs of these homes, the homes' profitability and the average total profit for each year.

Once an underwriter finishes reviewing a loan, the entire investment risk is evaluated. Under many lending policies, if one aspect of the transaction fails to meet program guidelines, the underwriter may be permitted to identify other criteria that exceed the minimum qualifications and use it as a compensating factor. Any such credit decision will be based on compensation factors and must be clearly documented in the underwriting worksheet.

In summary, the underwriter analyzes a wide variety of documents and requirements to ensure loan compliance, and generally additional information from the borrower is needed to complete the review. Ultimately, underwriting concludes with a lending recommendation – to approve or disapprove.

Denying a Loan

Under the Fair Credit Reporting Act, lenders are required to notify borrowers of the reason(s) a loan may be declined. If an underwriter denies a loan, borrowers and loan officers may have various options to save the loan, depending on the reason for disapproval. Typically, the loan officer speaks directly to the loan applicant to discuss reasons why the loan was not approved and explores options for restructuring the transaction. In this case, the loan amount may be changed or additional documentation may be required.

Whatever the solution for restructuring the loan, the lender will specify a deadline for receipt in order for the underwriting process to resume.

Review

1. What do lenders avoid when discussing a builder review with their loan applicant?

_____

_____

_____

2. What are the two methods used by appraisers for estimating the value of a property?

_____

_____

_____

3. A collateral review takes what specific documents into consideration?

_____

_____

_____

4. What happens during loan processing?

_____

_____

_____

5. What are several reasons why an underwriter might decline a loan?

_____

_____

_____

"There is only one boss – The customer.

And he can fire everybody in the company from the chairman on down simply by spending his money somewhere else."

~ Sam Walton

Module #4:

Closing Phase

Objectives

- ☐ Understand the importance of the closing phase
- ☐ Recognize the different components of the closing phase
- ☐ Identify how the closing phase benefits the other phases

Introduction

Once the underwriting process is completed and approved, a closing agent finalizes the loan. During the "closing" process, all of the construction loan agreements and legally binding documents are executed, and all instructions for processing the agreements and distributing funds are implemented. Depending on the state where the mortgaged property is located, closing services are provided by attorneys, title companies or escrow companies. Upon closing the loan, the borrower holds the lender responsible for performing their obligations, which include making disbursements under the terms of the loan.

If the land or lot (where construction is to occur) is owned free and clear by the borrower, the loan closing is somewhat simplified. However, if the borrower is purchasing the land or needs to pay off a prior mortgage with a portion of the construction loan proceeds, payoff of the seller or prior lender must occur concurrently with the close of the construction loan. These concurrent transactions add many additional steps to the closing process.

Cash In and Out of Escrow

During the closing of the mortgage, the borrower and lender incur numerous costs in the course of negotiating, underwriting and closing processes of the construction loan. All of these expenses must be paid at closing. The lender might also require the borrower to pay certain origination fees or offer rebate fees back to the borrower.[9] Additional fees might include a funding fee and a document drawing fee as well as paying the costs of notarizing

---

[9] Lenders usually offer borrowers a range of interest rate options from which they can choose. Borrowers might want to pay "discount points" to the lender in order to reduce their interest rate. These fees are called 'points' because they are usually expressed in terms of percentage points of the mortgage amount. If no discount points are paid or rebated, the borrower will have opted for the interest rate "at par." Sometimes lenders will rebate fees back to the borrower in exchange for the borrower to accept a higher interest rate. Circumstances occur where it can benefit the borrower to pay discount points in order to "buy down" their interest rate, especially if they plan to keep the home or they are financing and making payments on the mortgage for a long period of time. It can also benefit the borrower to accept a higher interest rate in return for a rebate of points from the lender, i.e., the borrower needs additional cash to close the loan.

and recording various documents. Further payments from the borrower encompass the services of a closing agent and title insurer as well as credit report and an appraisal report fees.

If the land/lot is purchased at closing, a check for the purchase proceeds is sent to the seller. If the seller decides to pay a portion of the current year's property taxes, the buyer is required to reimburse the seller for the taxes applicable to the portion of the current tax year. If either the property seller or the current borrower already owns a mortgage on the property, a payoff check is executed, including accrued unpaid interest, and it is sent to the mortgage holder at closing. The mortgagee collects a fee for issuing a payoff demand statement to the closing agent.

Prior to actually closing the loan, the closing agent gathers the funds to pay these parties. Often, some of these payments are included in the new loan, or the borrower is required to pay all of them out of pocket. The lender's ability to include all of the fees in the loan is limited by the lender's maximum loan to value ratio (LTV). LTV expresses the ratio of a loan to the value of an asset purchased and equals the loan amount divided by the lesser of appraised value or purchase price of the property. The lender may have a maximum LTV on the unimproved property on the day the loan closes and will certainly have a maximum LTV on the completed construction project with the loan fully disbursed. Any shortfall that exists between the disbursed loan portion on the day the loan closes and the total amount of cash needed at closing is the amount the borrower must contribute. In other words, this is the borrower's "cash to close." If the borrower agrees to pay a portion of the construction costs out of their own pocket, the lender will require this amount prior to disbursing loan funds. Otherwise, the borrower's funds will be held and disbursed prior to, or concurrently with, the loan funds.

Down Payments and Borrower Equity

The term *'down payment'* is generically used to describe the borrower's equity in the property. In cases where the borrower purchases the property and the lender is unwilling to fund 100 percent of the land purchase, the borrower's down payment will equal the difference between the purchase price and the portion the lender is financing. In this circumstance, the down payment might be a large component of the borrower's cash to close.

If a borrower already owns a portion of the land under construction, free of encumbrances, this holding interest serves as their down payment. Generally, lenders prefer borrowers that invest their own money into a construction project long before the project is complete. From a lender's perspective, equity at closing, whether pre-existing equity or from a down payment, serves two purposes. Since the mortgage gives the lender the right to foreclose on the property in the event of a borrower default, equity provides the borrower an incentive to comply with the terms of the loan agreements in order to protect the investment. If the borrower does default, equity provides a cushion between the outstanding loan amount and the property value to help cover the costs of foreclosure and liquidation by the lender.[10]

---

[10] In practice, the value of a property in foreclosure is often insufficient to repay the loan in full and cover the costs of foreclosure and liquidation. Foreclosures frequently result in a loss to the lender. Thus, contrary to

Documents, Closing and Final Settlement

In advance of closing the loan, numerous documents are required, and all are circulated for signatures by various parties. Multiple documents must be notarized[11] and recorded with the county, including deeds and mortgages at the time that they are signed. Once all of the documents and cash-to-close are in the possession of the closing agent, the information is verified and reviewed, and the closing agent then asks the lender to deposit any loan funds at closing. These funds will be remitted to the closing agent electronically via the Federal Reserve's wire system. The lender employee who verifies all of the documentation and disburses the loan proceeds to the closing agent is called the Funder.

Once the required documents, cash and loan proceeds are in the agent's possession, the closing is ready to proceed. Legally, all of the tasks required for the final closing take place concurrently at the beginning of business on the day of closing. This timing minimizes risk and ensures that large payments are received by the lender and reciprocated by the borrower, who will become the new owner. At the time of closing, the seller receives the purchase price concurrently with the deed to the borrower being recorded. The prior mortgage holder receives their payoff simultaneously with the new mortgage, allowing the new mortgagee the first mortgage holder in the line of title. If a portion of the loan is disbursed at closing, it is completed all together with the recording of the new mortgage, allowing the disbursed funds to be secured by the collateral property. The title insurer dates the title policy to be concurrent with the recording of the new mortgage; thus, no time lapse occurs between the date of the mortgage and the date when the title coverage becomes effective.

The table on the next page lists the major documents and tasks required for closing a construction loan:

---

some people's beliefs, the lender does not want your house! Lenders would much prefer borrowers comply with their loan agreements and avoid the prospect of foreclosure altogether.

[11] Notarization is the process of certifying a document through a notary public, who is constituted by law to serve the public. The notary public verifies the identify of individuals signing the document, witnesses the signatures and marks the document with a stamp of 'seal.'

Major Documents Required for Closing a Construction Loan

What Is It?	What Does the Closing Agent Do With It?
Promissory Note *The promissory note evidences the borrower's promise to repay the loan. It also spells out the amount borrowed, the interest rate, terms of any rate/payment adjustments, the amount and due date of monthly payments, and the late charge amount, if not paid on time.*	*This document is drawn by the lender and forwarded to the closing agent. The closing agent executes it for the borrower and then returns it to the lender. Promissory notes are negotiable instruments, meaning they can be sold. Therefore, lenders need to keep them in a secure location.*
New Mortgage or Deed of Trust *The new mortgage or deed of trust demonstrates the borrower's granting to the lender of a security interest in the collateral property. It includes a legal description of the property and discusses the borrower's responsibility to maintain the property and keep property taxes and insurance current. It also spells out the lender's right to inspect the property and to foreclose if the borrower fails to fulfill any of their obligations in any of the agreements between borrower and lender.*	*This document is drawn by the lender and forwarded to the closing agent. The closing agent executes it for the borrower, notarizes it and sends it to the County for recording on the closing date. After recording, the County Recorder returns it to the lender.*
Construction Loan Agreement *The construction loan agreement specifies the conditions to be met in order to receive construction loan funds, the method for requesting funds and the method of disbursing funds. It usually indicates the lender has a right to inspect the construction progress and to examine the condition of title to the property before each disbursement is released. It also cites duties of the borrower and builder according to plans and specifications*	*This document is drawn by the lender and forwarded to the closing agent. The closing agent executes it for the borrower and then returns it to the lender.*
New Loan Proceeds and Borrower's Cash to Close *The new loan proceeds and borrower's cash to close itemize any of the construction loan proceeds that are to be disbursed at closing. These proceeds will be deposited with the closing agent by the lender's funder. Borrower's cash to close is also deposited with the closing agent by the borrower.*	*Proceeds are disbursed by the closing agent according to the lender's instruction. Instructions could include sending payoff proceeds to the mortgagee on land being purchased or refinanced, sending purchase proceeds directly the seller of land with no mortgage on it or disbursing construction proceeds to the borrower or the builder. Other instructions could include reimbursing a seller for prepaid property taxes, paying the title policy premium, paying for recording fees and many, many others.*

Major Documents Required for Closing a Construction Loan

What Is It?	What Does the Closing Agent Do With It?
Title Insurance Policy *The title insurance policy is used to obtain a preliminary title policy prior to approving the loan. After approval of the loan, the lender then secures a commitment from the title insurer to issue the final policy upon recordation of the mortgage or deed of trust.*	*Upon notification that the mortgage or deed of trust has been recorded, the title insurer issues the policy directly to the lender, usually within a few weeks.*
Payoff to Seller of Land *A payoff to seller of land contract is a contract between a seller and a buyer where the purchase price is agreed upon between all parties involved.*	*This document is disbursed by the closing agent at closing according to buyer's, seller's or lender's instructions depending on the source of the funds. Seller will only receive funds after any mortgage on the sold property is paid off.*
Deed from Seller to Buyer *The deed from seller to buyer is a document that conveys ownership from seller to buyer*	*This document is drafted by the closing agent, executed by the seller, and notarized and recorded by the closing agent upon closing.*
Payoff of Prior Mortgage *The payoff to prior mortgage satisfies the mortgage on the property being sold or refinanced in full. Satisfaction of the prior mortgage allows the new mortgage to be the first mortgage in the chain of title.*	*Upon closing, this document is disbursed by the closing agent in accordance with the new lender's instructions.*
Rescission or Release of Prior Mortgage *Rescission or release of prior mortgage removes a paid off mortgage from title to the property.*	*This document is prepared and recorded by the mortgagee who has been reimbursed. Most states have laws that specify the mortgagee has a certain amount of time to release their mortgage after payoff. If they fail to do so, a property owner or title company has the right to do it themselves. (Attempting to record a release of a mortgage that <u>has not</u> been satisfied in full will almost certainly result in legal action being initiated by the mortgagee or a public prosecutor.)*
Closing Disclosure *The closing disclosure is a statement of actual charges and adjustments paid by the borrower and the seller, to be given to the parties in connection with the settlement and presented to the borrower at loan closing.*	*This document is required to be given by a lender to the borrower at least three business days before closing the loan. This three-day window allows the borrower time to compare final terms and costs to those estimated in the Loan Estimate. The three days also gives borrowers time to ask the lender any questions before closing.*

The functions and responsibilities of a closing agent are numerous and sundry as they coordinate the final steps of a construction purchase. Closing agents ensure all documents and paperwork are managed appropriately, and parties of the closing transaction place a great deal of trust in the agent to properly handle important legal agreements and large sums of money.

The consequences of mishandling a closing are serious and could bring about the loss of property, money, legal rights, and more. Many lawsuits have been filed against closing agents who failed to follow sound business practices. Because of the complexity of these real estate transactions, closing agents employ highly skilled, experienced and closely supervised personnel in an effort to avoid errors. As such, closing agents must be licensed and insured in many states or bonded against errors, omissions and acting in bad faith.

Review

1. Who provides closing services for lenders?

   _____

   _____

   _____

2. What is the meaning of "cash to close?"

   _____

   _____

   _____

3. What events happen concurrently in a loan closing? Why?

   _____

   _____

   _____

4. What are some of the sources and uses of funds deposited with the closing agent? How do they account for these funds?

   _____

   _____

   _____

5. What is the difference between a promissory note and a mortgage? What does the closing agent do with these documents?

_____

_____

_____

Module #5:

Post-Closing Phase

Objectives

- ☐ Recognize the components of the post-closing phase
- ☐ Identify the steps for successful loan administration
- ☐ Master troubled assets
- ☐ Understand loan modifications

Introduction to Post-Closing Phase

Post-closing is one of the most important steps in the construction loan process. Once the loan has closed, the one-time close post-closing process begins by the borrower requesting "draws" or disbursements of construction funding. At this point, loan officers, processors, underwriters and other loan origination personnel are no longer involved. Instead, the loan administration team supports and fulfills the lender's obligations under the loan agreement. The lender closely monitors the project to ensure the borrower is fulfilling the required commitments, including the agreements to build according to specifications and to protect the collateral from damage or deterioration. If the borrower is in compliance with the agreement, the lender must disburse funds as requested.

Once the loan administrator starts disbursing funds, a precise accounting of the amounts must be managed to complete the construction of budgeted line items for all funds disbursed. Until progress and compliance of the loan agreement is confirmed from the borrower and builder, the lender may withhold each draw request. During this process, lenders possess great leverage, demanding performance from each party. The borrower requires loan proceeds to build the new home, and the builder depends on loan funding to pay employees and suppliers and make a profit and stay in business. Loan administrators understand time is of the essence, so they are prepared to verify compliance and disburse funds as quickly and efficiently as possible. Unnecessary delays due to inefficient loan administration may cause frustration and friction among borrowers, builders and material suppliers, which may turn performing loans into troubled assets

Necessary Terms and Components to Understand Post-Closing

- **Initial Post-Close Meeting:** A meeting with the borrower to ensure he or she understands the mechanics of the construction phase. This includes how to obtain construction funds, tips for keeping the project running smoothly and the importance of completing on time.
- **Initial Draw:** The first release of money from the loan to begin construction. This draw normally covers permits, architect, and/or site preparation costs.

- **Subsequent Draws:** Additional releases of loan funds which occur after the initial draw and prior to the final draw. These draws make up the majority of the post-closing phase.
- **Final Draw:** Typically accounts for 10 percent of the total fund where the lender issues a check jointly payable to the borrower and the builder.
- **Appraisal Update and/or Completion Report (1004D):** Confirmation that the project was completed as originally represented to the lender and understood by the original appraiser.
- **Troubled Assets:** Loans where borrowers, builders and/or collateral are seriously out of compliance with the loan agreements. Troubled assets can also be defined as other problems that have arisen in the loan process and pose a potential loss to the lender.
- **Modification:** Changing the original terms of any loan agreement. The lender may grant modifications as a courtesy to the borrower because of benefits to the lender, such as permitting construction to continue and avoiding a loan default.
- **Conversion to Permanent Financing:** Transition from the construction phase to the permanent financing phase.

Initial Post-Close Meeting

Immediately after closing the loan, the loan administration team contacts the borrower and explains the process for requesting and obtaining funds, as detailed in the loan agreements. Typically, the draw schedule of work is discussed, which is the detailed payment plan for the construction project. The lender provides a draw request form to the borrower for the disbursement of funds and describes what paper or electronic forms are required for completion. A growing number of lenders also provide borrowers with user credentials to a lender web site, where the borrower can request funds.

Equally important, the loan administrator explains additional items to supply with each draw (the 'draw request package,') including all of the required steps and the associated timelines for processing a draw. The administrator confirms how (check/wire), where (address/account/routing number) and to whom (borrower/borrower representative/builder, borrower and builder) draw funds will be delivered to the borrower. Finally, a contact list with names, phone numbers and e-mail addresses is provided if he or she has questions or encounters any problems.

Initial Draw

When the borrower or builder requests the first draw, actual construction might already be under way. Moreover, the borrower and their builder may be asking for deposits or start-up money in order to begin work (see Budget Shortfall/Over-Disbursement under Troubled Assets (page 53) later in this module for more information).

From the lender's point of view, several items should be collected and reviewed prior to releasing the initial draw including draw request form, waivers, permits, builder's risk insurance, inspection (if required).

Draw Request Form

The draw request form and the progress inspection (draw inspection) are the most important forms of communication between the borrower, builder and lender. The draw request form acts as the borrower and builder's statement to the lender for needed funds, explaining the portion of the loan proceeds which they are entitled. The lender responds with a progress inspection, detailing construction development and allocating the appropriate loan proceeds to the borrower and builder accordingly. It is imperative that the borrower, builder and lender agree on the issue of loan fund entitlement at each draw, so no party perceives funds are being unreasonably withheld.

Most lenders and several government sponsored loan programs retain and manage their own, customized draw request forms. In like manner, trade organizations, such as the American Institute of Architects, provide their members with standardized, example draw request forms.

At a minimum, the form must contain the following information:

- Identification of the borrower and the project including the loan number
- Date of the draw request
- A line item cost breakdown of each construction element provided by the lender including (e.g. permits, rough grading, ground plumbing, foundation, framing labor and materials, roofing, exterior doors/windows, rough mechanical systems, etc., all the way to final cleaning and touch up)
- The total amount agreed to by the lender for financing
- The full amount the borrower is seeking with the current draw request

The following components are also extremely helpful:

- Lender's dollar and percentage amount of each line item already disbursed and the remaining amounts to be disbursed
- Lender's last date of inspection and the percentage completion for each line item
- Lender's overall percentages of disbursement and completion
- Lender's summary of any changes to the original budget including additional advances or re-allocation of line items
- Borrower's and builder's assertions that all information is correct and all work for current and previous draw requests has been submitted and completed in accordance with plans and specs

Permits

Many construction lenders require an issued building permit prior to the loan closing. If the borrower does not provide this permit, (assuming they are required by local ordinance), the loan administrator must obtain it prior to releasing the initial draw. Without obtaining required permits, any construction is deemed illegal and only the unimproved land technically secures any loan disbursements for improvements.

Builder's Risk Insurance

Builder's risk insurance is defined as "coverage that protects a person's or organization's insurable interest in materials, fixtures and/or equipment used in a construction project or structure should those items sustain physical loss or damage from a covered cause." Similar to homeowner's insurance, builder's risk insurance protects against the loss of property due to fire, natural disasters, vandalism, theft, etc. It also extends homeowner's coverage to materials and fixtures that are in the process of being incorporated into the permanent improvements. This coverage typically applies to any materials and fixtures physically located on the project site, and in some cases, it pertains to components in transit to the construction location. Equipment and items purchased and stored at an off-site storage facility should be covered and insured by the policy at that location or by the entity in control of the facility. In these cases, the borrower, not the builder, is named as the insured, and the lender is named as the loss co-payee. Subsequently, if the lost or damaged property was originally purchased using loan proceeds, the lender can control whether insurance benefits would be used to replace the property or pay down the loan. The builder's risk coverage typically terminates once the property is ready for occupancy. Once this occurs, standard homeowner's coverage is purchased.

During the pre-closing phase, most lenders request proof of a builder's risk coverage since it is frequently issued in the form of an endorsement to a homeowner's policy, without which the lender may not fund the loan. The same is true of flood insurance if the property is located in an area determined to be a special hazard flood area as specified by the Federal Emergency Management Administration (FEMA). To confirm coverage is in place, the lender must check the expiration dates of these policies with each draw. If a policy has expired, the lender will insist that the borrower provides proof of coverage renewal prior to disbursing funds.

Following are additional types of insurance a lender may require prior to releasing funds:

- General Liability: Covers financial risk in the case of bodily injury or property damage to others. In most states, general liability insurance is a critical form of coverage and secures a contractor's license. This form of insurance is intended to settle reasonable claims of loss caused by the builder, provided that the category and cause of loss are covered under the policy.

- Workers' Compensation Insurance: Provides contractor's employees with coverage for lost wages and medical expenses resulting from workplace accidents.

- Errors and Omissions: Used to settle reasonable claims of loss caused by the builder's negligence, in the case of failure to perform or providing faulty professional advice.

- Surety Bond: Guarantees a certain sum payment from a lender to the builder's client (the borrower) if the builder fails to perform their obligations. Often prohibitively expensive, a surety bond's premium costs between one percent and three percent of the total bond amount. Applicants with increased personal risk, such as smaller builders, can anticipate even higher rates.

Survey and/or Foundation Endorsement

Early in a construction project timeline, the actual building footprint and location is established on site by staking the corners of a basement, foundation footings or a slab on grade, depending on the building design. A lender must be cognizant of the builder's placement, ensuring it is placed exactly where approved plans indicate it should be. If not, property owners and lenders face the risk and added expense of physically relocating a building or tearing it down to reconstruct it elsewhere. Consequently, lenders regularly employ a land surveyor to visit the site and physically measure the location of the improvements relative to property boundaries, required setbacks and easements.

In lieu of directly ordering a survey, a foundation endorsement may be purchased from the original title insurer. Providing assurance to the lender, this order certifies the land designated for construction is within the correct boundaries and does not encroach onto easements or violate particular covenants, conditions, or restrictions listed in the title policy exceptions. However, the foundation endorsement may not address whether the improvements comply with building setback requirements.

The title company may require a survey prior to issuing the endorsement or may waive the survey requirement and issue coverage at its own risk. Lenders must understand the terms of coverage and determine if they require additional assurances to guarantee the building improvements are correctly situated.

Mechanic's Lien Waivers

A *lien waiver* is a signed statement or document from a contractor, subcontractor, or supplier explaining that, subject to some conditions, he or she will refrain from exercising the right to place a mechanic's lien on the property. As discussed previously, a subcontractor may file a mechanic's lien on properties where construction has occurred and the contractor asserts she was not paid as originally agreed.

Mechanic's lien laws vary from state to state, but generally, without a detailed analysis by an attorney, loan administrators deem the priority of a mechanic's lien to date back to the time labor and materials were supplied. Consequently, all or a portion of the construction loan proceeds could be subordinated to the mechanic's lien, and the person filing the lien is entitled to payment from the property sale proceeds before the lender is reimbursed. In some cases, the 'claimant,' or filer of the lien can force a sale of the property in order to be compensated.

When a mechanic's lien is filed, it is advisable to stop disbursing construction funds until the lien is resolved (see Troubled Assets – Mechanic's Liens later in this module.) In order to minimize risk of mechanic's liens, the lender and borrower must receive mechanic's lien waivers from recipients of construction loan proceeds each time they are paid.

Following are several types of lien waivers:

Interim Draws:

- Conditional Waiver and Release Upon Progress Payment: States that as of a certain date, a specific sum is due. Upon receipt of payment, the contractor releases his right to place a lien. A conditional waiver should be required with each draw as it relates to the current request for funds if the contractor is not comfortable providing an Unconditional Waiver and Release Upon Progress Payment. The draw amount funded by the lender should match the amount noted on the lien waiver.

- Unconditional Waiver and Release Upon Progress Payment: Asserts that as of a certain date, the contractor releases his right to place a lien without condition. The unconditional waiver, as it relates to all previously received funds, should be required with each draw. This should be considered the preferred lien waiver during the interim draw process if the contractor is willing to execute.

Final Draw:

- Conditional Waiver and Release Upon Final Payment: Affirms that as of a certain date, a specific sum is due for payment in full under the building contract. Upon receipt of final payment; the contractor releases his right to place a lien. The conditional waiver should be required with the final request for funds if the contractor is not comfortable providing an Unconditional Waiver and Release Upon Final Payment. The final draw amount funded by the lender should match the amount noted on the lien waiver.

- Unconditional Waiver and Release Upon Final Payment: Explains that as of a certain date, the contractor releases his right to place a lien without condition. The final unconditional waiver must be requested from the payee after the final payment has been released and has cleared the payee's bank. Once the payment has been received, the lender has no further inducement to obtain the release. For this reason, some lenders require this lien release prior to making the final disbursement. Many contractors are not comfortable signing this lien waiver without being funded first. A Conditional Waiver and Release Upon Final Payment is a viable alternative in those instances.

Mechanic's Lien Endorsement

Within the mechanic lien process, construction lenders often obtain a mechanic's lien endorsement to the original title policy prior to each release of funds. Ordered directly from the title company, this document is issued after the title company re-examines the condition of title. It also states whether any mechanic's liens have been recorded against the property and whether any new release of funds would be subordinated (see Troubled Assets – Mechanic's Liens in this module.)

Draw (Progress) Inspection

A draw inspection is a type of inspection that provides a visual observation of progress on a construction project, normally completed by a professional inspector and on behalf of the lender. Before lenders release construction funds, they must certify the work has been completed for funds that are being requested. By confirming the budget at the line item level, lenders manage the overall percentage of disbursement in parity with the overall percentage of completion, ensuring construction funds are not depleted until construction is 100 percent finished.

To this end, lenders send inspectors to the properties to determine if the draw request form accurately reflects what the borrower and builder are claiming. In addition to the draw request form, the lender must provide a complete line item cost breakdown to the inspector, demonstrating the amount of money funded for each item and the percentage completed from the previous inspection. Inspectors also examine all materials on site, ensuring they are properly stored, as stated by the lenders' policies and material storage requirements.

The inspector finalizes a report and returns it to the lender, furnishing written data and photographic evidence and noting each line item and its respective percentage completed. This documentation assists the lender to determine how much of the borrower's fund request is actually eligible to be disbursed.

To determine the progress of construction and the associated funding, lenders may contract directly with a draw inspector or use a vendor management company, who manages the draw inspection process and completes the report. Vendor management companies should provide lenders additional insurance coverage as well as centralized scheduling, order and web site tracking, standard proactive communication, compliance management, technology integration, data retention, and a consolidated quality control process. A valuable vendor management company also offers wide geographic coverage and inspection services in areas seldom served by the lender. To perform draw inspections on single-family homes, it is best to use inspectors with hands-on construction experience, so they understand management and development of a single-family residence.

For further information on draw inspections and the stages of home construction, Trinity Real Estate Solutions offers a step-by-step book entitled *Introduction to Residential Draw Inspections*. This book includes photographs and descriptions describing every step of the construction process.

Architectural Approval

Some communities require contractual review and approval on a property's architectural approval and quality of site design. This review examines the structure's compliance to community-imposed conditions and restrictions, as they pertain to aesthetic standards. As with permits, no construction funds should be released until any required architectural approvals have been obtained. Otherwise, the community could potentially force the owner to demolish loan-funded improvements and potentially leave the lender inadequately secured by the collateral.

Subsequent Draws

Once a construction project's first draw is completed, the routine of processing subsequent draws continues as construction progresses. The construction loan agreement may specifically limit the number of draws allowed over the life of the construction project. Otherwise, the agreement states draws can occur on a defined frequency, such as once per month. While lenders incur administrative expenses to process draw requests, such as paying loan administrators' salaries, a specific amount of loan proceeds are allocated to pay for progress inspections.

A loan administrator's key objective involves keeping construction progressing smoothly. This includes processing draws efficiently while preventing any friction between borrowers, contractors and lenders. Ultimately, loan administrators are responsible for enforcing the terms of the loan agreements and ensuring the entire customer base is well served.

With each subsequent draw, the borrower submits the current draw request form along with any conditional and unconditional lien releases for all previous draws. Upon receipt of a request, the loan administrator verifies the current loan status (interest payments current, etc.) and all contractors' licenses and insurance coverages ensuring they are not expired. Any lapsed licenses or insurance should be renewed before proceeding with the request. The loan administrator then orders the progress inspection and the mechanic's lien endorsement. Once the inspection and endorsement are received and reviewed, funds are disbursed to the borrower or builder in amounts up to the percentage of completion of each individual line item as indicated on the progress inspection.

Final Draw

Eventually, if all goes as planned and the construction project reaches its conclusion, the borrower begins seeking all undisbursed funds remaining in the loan. As a common practice, many lenders practice a term entitled 'retention,' which refers to postponing 10 percent of each requested draw amount from the original construction contract. The lender withholds this amount as an inducement to the builder to complete every detail of the work described in the plans and specifications. Once the final progress inspection is returned and each line item states 100 percent completion, a "Certificate of Occupancy" is issued by the municipality, if applicable, with the final draw request and the full amount due to the building contractor.

Some lenders require a letter from the homeowner stating the house is completed to their satisfaction. This method protects lenders from subsequent borrower claims, stating the lender disbursed remaining funds to the builder prior to 100 percent completion. Typically, if disbursement checks are issued directly to the builder, the final draw check will be distributed jointly payable to the builder and the homeowner. If lenders take this precaution, the homeowners have an opportunity to withhold their endorsement of the check until any minor, agreed upon construction is completed. The Conditional/Unconditional Waiver and Release upon Final Payment should also accompany the final draw request, as predicated by the lender's policy.

Appraisal Update and/or Completion Report

Most lenders (and some government loan programs) require certification of a property via a real estate appraiser, verifying the original design of the structure. The "1004D" by Fannie Mae and the "442" by Freddie Mac[12] are the standard forms used for these appraisals with two intended purposes.

1. An appraiser uses the Summary Appraisal Report Update to explain the validated increase or decrease of value for the completed property since its original appraisal in the pre-construction phase.

2. Certification of Completion (not to be confused with the local government-issued Certificate of Occupancy) states the structure either has or has not been completed in accordance with the requirements and conditions (room count, size, design, amenities, etc.) as indicated in the pre-construction appraisal report.

Under several loan programs, a mortgage cannot be converted to a permanent mortgage and sold in the secondary market without one or both of these reports.

Troubled Assets

Troubled assets are goods that financial institutions have overpaid causing financial loss to the lender. These resources consist of assets that fail to perform according to the terms of the note, the mortgage and the construction loan agreement.

The most famous example of troubled assets includes subprime mortgages, which lost much of their value and became almost impossible to sell when the real estate market collapsed in 2007-2008.

Following are descriptions of non-performance mortgage issues during the construction phase:

Budget Shortfall/Over-Disbursement – Budget shortfalls occur when insufficient funds are available to complete an aspect of the project on a construction budget line item. One example might involve a framing budget shortfall. In this case, a lack of funds exists in a line item to pay for the labor and materials for framing a house. Conversely, over-disbursement translates into a percentage of disbursement of a line item exceeding the percentage of completion. Continuing with the example, if the framing of the house is only 50 percent complete but the framing budget line equals 60 percent disbursed, framing would be considered 10 percent over-disbursed.

Budget shortfall and over-disbursement are two sides of the same coin, indicating that in both cases, funds are being depleted faster than work is being completed.

---

[12] Fannie Mae or FNMA stands for Federal National Mortgage Association. Freddie Mac or FHLMC stands for Federal Home Loan Mortgage Corporation. These organizations are U.S. government sponsored enterprises, created to promote liquidity in the secondary mortgage market. The secondary market refers to the mechanism by which lenders sell pools of mortgages to investors in order to free up capital to originate more loans.

In some cases, a line item can be over-disbursed temporarily. If a borrower is asked by their builder to pay bills which cause a line item to be over-disbursed by a few percentage points, it is prudent to accommodate the request to preserve the borrower-builder relationship. Deposits for expensive items, such as framing materials, cabinetry, doors and windows, require large outlays of capital before these items can be delivered to the job site.

During a budget shortfall or over-disbursement, communication between all parties is a critical component. If funds are repetitively requested well ahead of the percentage of line item completion, representatives must ask for an explanation and use sound judgment.

Loan administrators must watch for over-disbursed line items that persist over multiple inspections. If a deposit for kitchen cabinets causes a line item to be over-disbursed, the next inspection will likely show a percentage of completion for cabinet installation quickly catching up to the percentage of disbursement. If not, ask the borrower and the builder for an explanation. Persistent over-disbursements could be an indicator of insufficient funding for that budget line item within the construction project. The borrower may not possess the expertise to understand budget insufficiencies, and the builder may not address the potential issue. A progress inspector should assess the situation to complete the work. If not, it's time to have a very candid conversation with the borrower as to where they will obtain the additional funds for completion.

Inactivity – Construction loan agreements must contain specific completion dates. For a twelve-month construction loan term, lenders expect to see regular draw requests and progress inspections, which steadily reflect progress towards completion. By the third month, a project typically reflects a 25 percent completion rate, 50 percent at the project's halfway point and 100 percent complete at month twelve. If lenders do not see regular draw requests and advancement with increasing completion percentages, they should contact their borrowers to understand if progress is halted.

Weather delays are another common reason for inactivity, often occurring during winter months. It is less common for borrowers and builders to use their own funds for construction without quickly asking for reimbursement. If work stops due to a contractor's inability to perform, failure to pass a critical inspection, or some unforeseen site condition preventing progress, the lender must be notified as soon as possible. In these cases, steps can be taken to protect the collateral, establish the cause of the problem and work with the borrower to create a solution. If clear explanations are not available, a progress inspector can assess development and assist in determining next steps.

Delinquency/Interest Reserve Depletion – Many construction loans include interest reserves, which the borrower can draw upon during the construction phase. Interest reserves are especially convenient for borrowers, who may lack the resources to make mortgage payments, pay rent on their current place of residence and concurrently owe on a home under construction. Interest reserves are included in the line item cost breakdown, and they are calculated to be sufficient to pay monthly interest on a growing loan balance over the construction term.

If the project experiences protracted delays after the loan closing or a long period of inactivity, the interest reserve could be depleted before construction is complete. In this instance, the loan will become delinquent[13]. Interest delinquency is the most common form

---

[13] "Delinquency" is simply defined as a payment that has not been tendered to the lender at the time that it is

of default on mortgage loans, and when this occurs, lenders must quickly reach out to their borrowers and attempt to formulate a plan to remedy the default. Otherwise, the lender must call the loan immediately due and payable, likely resulting in a foreclosure. If the house is not already in an advanced state of completion, the lender will likely experience a financial loss.

Casualty Loss – A host of issues can damage a building or structure, including fire, theft, vandalism, wind damage, flooding, and structural failure, whether it's under construction, completed and occupied. When damage occurs, one of the in-place insurance policies should cover the loss, whether it's builder's risk, general liability, or another option. The lender is typically named as the loss co-payee on any policy that protects against damage to the property and will receive funds for reconstructing any portion of the building with loss or damage. Under the terms of the mortgage, the lender maintains the right to hold the funds and disburse them as if they were construction funds from the original loan. The lender can "repack" the line items for the lost/damaged property or keep them in a separate escrow account and disburse them to the borrower as requested. This way, an inspection will confirm that repairs are being completed and reimbursed as needed. In the event of a total loss, the lender or borrower will opt to pay down the loan balance and cancel the construction altogether. If the borrower is unable to quickly liquidate the property and pay off the outstanding loan balance, a technical default on the construction loan occurs.

Bankruptcy – Bankruptcy is a minefield of technical hazards. When a borrower or builder files bankruptcy, it is almost always in the lender's best interest to seek legal advice. A borrower bankruptcy is typically an event of default under the terms of the promissory note, and when it is filed, an "automatic stay" comes into effect, preventing any party from taking any action to collect a debt or exercise control over property of the estate. In this case, an owner or developer cannot attempt to collect debts owed by the bankrupt contractor without a court order. Bankruptcy legally prevents creditors from issuing verbal or written demands for repayment and repossessing property through foreclosure. If unspent loan proceeds are in the possession of any party when bankruptcy is filed, whether it's the builder or borrower, proceeds can be deemed to belong to the bankruptcy estate. A bankruptcy court then determines the disposition of those funds, which may or may not be in the lender's best interest.

Eventually, all bankruptcies are resolved in one of two courses of action:

1. They are discharged as a result of the borrower completing a reorganization of debts
2. They are dismissed due to the borrower's failing to work towards a resolution.

Within U.S Bankruptcy law, an *automatic stay* is an injunction that halts actions by the creditor to collect debts from the debtor. However, an automatic stay can be lifted for a particular creditor in order for them to seize collateral, perhaps for a foreclosing on real estate. In this case, the lender's attorney can advise the best manner to move forward when any of these remedies become available. As long as a party to the construction loan

---

contractually due. This applies to payments of interest, principal, taxes, insurance, or any sum that the loan agreements require a borrower to pay.

is in bankruptcy, it is ill advised to take any action against the borrower or any property in their possession, without first obtaining legal advice.

Mechanic's Liens – When mechanic's liens are filed, a lender should immediately stop disbursing funds and attempt to resolve the lien. Three potential resolutions are available for a lender:

1) Pay the lien to the claimant or person filing the lien.

   Initially, the lender must investigate whether the claimant is entitled to payment and whether there are funds.

2) Convince the claimant to rescind the lien.

   If the amount claimed is legitimate and funds are available, the lender must attempt to negotiate with both the borrower and builder to resolve the dispute, so payment can occur. If payments are not included in the loan, the borrower will need to find an alternative source of funds for payment. A negotiated lesser amount for the claimant might also be possible to avoid collection costs and legal action.

3) Sue for a court order to remove the lien.

   If funds for payment are unavailable, negotiations fail, or work claimed is not legitimate, the borrower must pursue legal action, which can be both expensive and time consuming for all parties involved.

If the borrower is unable or unwilling to execute one of these three options, the lender is left with a defaulted loan. Even if the lender forecloses, the lien may be found to take priority over all or a portion of the mortgage, so payment will occur from the liquidation proceeds of the foreclosed property.

Builder Replacement – Typically, the relationship between the builder and the borrower begins well because both have mutually chosen to work together. Unfortunately, the relationship may easily sour. Borrowers often experience stressful circumstances within the construction process, and they may not understand the intricacies and responsibilities of a builder. Conversely, a builder may believe the borrower is interfering with their work or making unreasonable demands. The builder may also be unable or unwilling to complete the construction due to lack of qualifications, competing demands upon their time, or an inability to develop congruous relationships with other parties on the job site. For these reasons, an impasse can occur between borrower and builder, and the selection of an alternative builder may be the only viable solution.

Selection of a replacement builder is no different from the enlistment, review and acceptance of the original builder (see Module 3 - Builder Review) with the exception of three additional complexities.

1) The exiting builder must be compensated for any amounts claimed by him. Otherwise, mechanics liens may be filed against the property (see Mechanic's Liens above.)
2) Locating an alternative builder willing to resume work-in-progress construction is extremely difficult. Many builders refuse to take on previously created construction

projects because of defect concerns.

3) The new builder must be willing to complete the project for whatever available funds remain (loan funds and borrower out-of-pocket funds) or a loan modification may be needed.

Although unfortunate, these complexities must be resolved in order for the lender to protect and preserve its overall investment.

Incapacitation of Borrower – Incapacitation of a borrower can occur by loss of a job, loss of one's good health or even loss of life. In the case of a loss of a job, construction should continue even though it may render him unable to make payments on a permanent mortgage once construction is complete. It is in the borrowers and lenders best interest to complete the house and sell it in order to repay the loan. Serious illness or death of the borrower requires a substitute individual, such as a spouse or estate executor, to assume an overseeing role for the project and authorize draws in the borrower's name to complete the house construction.

Loan Modification

A *loan modification* is technically defined as any alteration to the original terms of the construction loan. Routinely initiated by the borrower, a loan modification is a permanent change in one or more of the terms of a borrower's loan, allowing it to remain in place or be reinstated. This process usually results in a payment the borrower can afford.

Initially upon receipt of a modification request, a loan administrator must consider and determine who is authorized to underwrite and approve the modification. Otherwise, the lender's internal procedures may address authority and delegation for loan modifications. Eventually, the person who authorizes the modification will ensure they do so without contractually invalidating the lender's rights to enforce the terms of the loan. For this reason, modifications usually require approval of a senior officer within the lending organization.

The range of possibilities for modifications is infinite. Following are a sampling of the various modification requests expected with construction loans:

Extension – The most common modifications that occur within the construction agreement are extensions, so many lenders utilize a standardized extension modification form for their borrowers to sign at the beginning of the process. This form incorporates a new completion date into the original construction loan agreement.

In general, construction is an uncertain industry as periods of inactivity and slow progress often occur due to inclement weather, late material deliveries, scheduling conflicts among various trades, delays in scheduling permit inspections and a myriad of other factors. Many lenders use a rule of thumb to estimate the duration of a construction project by starting with the builder's time estimate for project completion, increasing it by 50 percent and rounding the result to the next highest multiple of three months. A reasonable term for home construction is six months, and interest reserves are based on this term[14]. If completion of construction takes longer, interest reserve will likely be exhausted. If the interest reserve is exhausted, the borrower will be required to make interest payments out of pocket as well as submit the monthly housing payment on the current place of residence.

Even with a reasonably calculated construction term, borrowers will often breach the original completion date and request more time. In these cases, many construction loan agreements specify that a fee be charged for each month of additional time requested. This fee may be expressed as a flat percentage of the fully disbursed note amount and may be charged as an incentive to the borrower. This action triggers the start of a project immediately after closing the loan in addition to ushering progress along. Of course, there will be times when an extension fee is waived because delays are caused by hardships, which can be out of the borrower's control.

Change Orders/Budget Reallocations – During the course of construction, borrowers and builders will inevitably discover that minor adjustments to the line item cost breakdown are necessary. Some items may be either over-budgeted or under-budgeted. Although this can be time consuming for loan administrators, it isn't necessarily problematic as long as the total loan amount does not change, and the plans and specifications for the house are not altered[15]. Carefully considering the total budget and various line items, the borrower should prepare a simple written request to the lender for any changes requesting "a decrease line item X of the budget and increase line item Y by the same amount." No actual modification of the loan documents would be necessary if the total loan amount remains the same.

Additional Advance – An additional advance is used by lenders to describe an increase in the construction loan amount. While borrowers may be tempted to add upgrades to their structures, it is advised to ensure they have the funding to pay for them. Unless the original loan-to-value ratio is well below loan program guidelines or the completed property value has increased since origination, lenders may not be able to increase the loan amount. The borrower must also qualify for the increased loan amount based on their credit score, cash reserves and capacity to make a larger monthly payment. All of these factors require a re-underwriting of the loan on some level. If all of these hurdles are crossed and the lender is willing to accommodate a request for a loan amount increase, the borrower must complete several factors:

- Execute a modification to the note
- Notarize a modification of the mortgage
- Pay for a title policy endorsement[16] to increase the coverage amount,

---

[14] For a discussion on calculating the interest reserve, see Module 2 under the heading "How does a Construction Loan Differ from a Permanent Mortgage?"

[15] Substantial changes to the plans and specifications could affect the value of a completed house, which could trigger a re-appraisal. If the value were to decline due to design changes, the entire loan could require renegotiation and execution.

[16] This endorsement would also reflect whether any new liens have appeared on title, such as mechanic's liens or junior mortgages. Any new lien holders would, at a minimum, have to agree to subordinate to the increase in the mortgage amount. If not, the lender will probably decline the request to increase their loan amount.

- Provide the lender with written instructions detailing the specifics for the allocation of additional funds.

Addition/Partial Release of Collateral – From time to time, borrowers approach lenders requesting a modification of their property description. If the borrower acquires new property adjacent to the mortgage property, lenders must not be concerned because the legal description of the mortgaged property will not change. However, if the borrower is releasing a portion of the mortgaged property to a new owner, the new owner is required to take title, subject to the mortgage unless the lender agrees to release it from the mortgage[17]. Lenders will generally be averse to a release of collateral unless it demonstrates it will not adversely affect the property value. This process typically requires a new appraisal, although some lot line adjustments between neighboring property owners can be so minor (e.g. not changing the total land area), the lender doesn't bother with a new evaluation. If the lender is satisfied, the borrower must execute and notarize a modification of the mortgage's legal description for the lender to record. The lender will then ask the title company to record it and modify the legal description in the title policy. Any land added to the legal description will be included on title as belonging to the borrower of record at the time of recordation.

Subordination/Consent to Easements – Borrowers will occasionally seek out the lender with a request to subordinate the mortgage to an easement. In many ways, this process can benefit the property. For example, granting a utility easement to bring water, power or natural gas to the property or granting an easement to widen a street in a residential area without bringing additional traffic is very beneficial. In these situations, lenders must use their own judgment to determine if an appraisal update is necessary. If they decide against a new appraisal, the lender simply executes and notarizes the subordination or partial release document and returns it to the borrower for their records. By consenting to the subordination, the lender constructively adds the land described in the document to the exceptions from title coverage.

Addition/Release of Borrower – A lender rarely permits the release of a borrower from a promissory note unless the remaining borrowers can demonstrate qualifications for the loan, credit authorization, and ability and capacity to repay the loan. An example of this type of loan release is in a divorce. In this case, one of two spouses is awarded sole ownership of a mortgaged property. Addition of borrowers is rare since there is little inducement for additional parties to oblige themselves to repay a loan after it has funded. The lender generally cannot require the addition of borrowers after a loan has funded. However, it is fairly common for a newly married borrower to place his or her new spouse on title to the property. This is accomplished by recording a deed and asking the lender to add the partner's name to his or her loan servicing records, authorizing the individual to obtain detailed information about the loan at will. Of course, the deed to the new spouse would be subordinated while having no bearing on the enforceability of the mortgage. Lenders commonly allow these types of 'intra-familial' transfers.

---

[17] Sale of a portion of the mortgaged property could constitute a breach of the due-on-sale clause of the mortgage, and the lender could declare the borrower to be in default of the mortgage agreement.

As discussed, many modification requests will require additional information gathering from a number of outside experts, including appraisers, attorneys, or title officers. A loan administrator should not attempt to modify a loan unless he or she has been explicitly authorized to so do by their employer because an improperly executed modification could seriously impair the enforceability of loan agreements and potentially lead to financial loss to the lender or the borrower.

Conversion to Permanent Financing

The final step in the post-closing construction phase is the conversion to permanent financing. As discussed previously, a two-time close loan requires the borrower to refinance the property and pay off the mortgage at the completion of construction. However, the one-time close construction loan encompasses both the construction phase, which generally spans six months to three years and the permanent financing phase for the mortgage, which can extend up to thirty years. Additionally, a great deal of variability between lenders' and loan programs occurs when transitioning between these phases. Much of that variability is driven by the lender's source of financing for the loan. A *portfolio loan* is a loan serviced by a lender with privately held cash and holds it as an asset on their company financial books. A *sold loan* is one that has been purchased from the lender on the secondary market.

The secondary mortgage market involves the practice of buying and selling home loans and servicing rights between mortgage lenders and investors. To a lender, a loan is an asset, and an asset is any item of value that can be sold. The value of the loan asset lays in the future payments of principal and the interest expected from the borrower. Investors will pay a price for those cash flows, depending on their size, expected timing, and perceived risk. Risk is a factor of the borrower's probability to pay as agreed, the adequacy of the collateral and the future expectations of higher or lower yielding future investments opportunities due to changes in interest rates. Lenders sell loans in the secondary market to gain a profit, and if they have done their job well, they will liquidate assets and generate cash to originate new loans. Secondary market investors review and scrutinize many terms before investment, including interest rates, loan amounts, credits quality, collateral adequacy, and more. Lenders must accommodate secondary market investors if they choose to liquidate their loans.

Many construction loans are eligible for sale into the secondary market at origination. These loans are fully disbursed at closing, and the construction funds are held in an investor's custodial bank account to be released to the borrower as draw requests are received. Borrowers will begin making monthly principal and interest payments on the full, principal balance from day one, and any unused construction funds at the end of the construction phase are used to pay down the loan balance. With the fulfillment of the construction phase, the lender notifies the investor that work is complete. At this point, the lender may or not be required to update or confirm the appraised value. For the borrowers, the conversion to permanent financing is seamless and transparent. The mortgagors simply continue to make monthly payments according to the terms of the note and begin enjoying their newly completed house.

If a lender holds the construction loan during both the construction phase and the permanent phase, he or she can define and determine arrangements with the borrower, which includes interest reserves, commencement of fully amortizing monthly payments, and modification of the terms of the note upon conversion to the permanent financing phase. If the loan and construction project were originally speculative in nature, and the borrower sold the house upon completion, no conversion to the permanent financing phase is needed. In this case, the borrower is required to sell the house and pay off the loan with the profits. These so-called "spec" loans are exclusively allowed for borrowers who demonstrate proficiency in real estate speculation or are professional builder or developers.

If the lender holds the construction loan in its portfolio and sells it in the secondary market upon completion of construction, the lender might allow the borrower to modify the terms of the loan for a number of reasons.

1) The loan is modified to prevent the borrower from refinancing with another lender, thereby precluding the construction lender from executing a profitable secondary market transaction.
2) The loan modification is revised to loan terms that are more favorable in the secondary market, as opposed to when the loan was originated.

These modifications pertain to the amount of interest payable on the note whether the interest rate is fixed or variable. Secondary market investors also require an appraisal update or a re-verification of any aspect of the credit file. If the collateral or the borrower's credit profile fails to qualify for a sale into the secondary market, the lender may have no choice but to retain the permanent mortgage in its portfolio. When lenders wait until completion of construction to sell a loan in the secondary market, they usually have a dedicated team of employees to convert the construction loans to permanent/sold loans because it requires detailed technical knowledge of investor requirements.

Review

1. During the post-closing phase, what is the lender's main job?

   _____

   _____

   _____

2. What is required to make the first draw?

   _____

   _____

   _____

3. What are lender risks when replacing a builder?

   _____

   _____

   _____

4. What should the lender review prior to releasing the final draw?

   _____

   _____

   _____

5. What is a troubled asset?

   _____

   _____

   _____

Review Answer Key

Module 2

1. A construction loan is a real estate financing tool that operates as a short-term commitment and typically ranges six months to three years in length. It is established by the borrower's 'Promise to Pay' and is secured by a mortgage on the property being financed. Loan proceeds are used to pay for land, labor and materials to construct a new building or improve an existing structure.
2. The similarities and differences between a construction and permanent mortgage include:
    Similarities: Both use a promissory note to provide the borrower's promise to pay and both are secured by real estate.
    Differences: A construction loan offers a short term span of time and is disbursed gradually as the building is erected. A permanent mortgage has a much longer term of up to 30 years and is distributed in full at origination. Additionally, construction loans are typically more expensive to acquire than permanent mortgages due to their complexity, additional exposed risk and higher interest rates.
3. **Two-Time Close**: A two-time close operates as two separate loans: a construction loan and a permanent mortgage. In this instance, two closings occur, and two sets of closing fees are expected for payment.
    One-Time Close: A one-time close requires only one loan and one closing process. The loan covers both the construction and the mortgage at the same time.
4. The borrower normally receives a better interest rate on a permanent mortgage versus a construction loan because the lender has access to more buyers in the secondary market for a permanent mortgage as opposed to a construction loan.
5. Construction loans create additional revenue sources for lenders because they are riskier in nature and command higher interest rates.

Module 3

1. Lenders avoid approving, endorsing or recommending a builder. The lender "accepts" or "registers" the builder chosen by the borrower because lenders are adverse to accepting liability for construction defects or other performance issues.
2. Two common methods used by appraisers for estimating the value of a property include:
    - Cost Approach
    - Sales Comparison Approach
3. A collateral review considers the appraisal and the contract.
4. During a loan process, documentation and data are compiled into a loan file for the underwriter to review.
5. An underwriter might decline a loan for insufficient borrower income or assets, ineligible collateral, or a non-qualified builder.

Module 4

1. Depending on the region of the country, closing services are provided by title companies, escrow companies and attorneys.
2. Cash to close is the difference between (a) the total loan proceeds and (b) the sum total of the property purchase price, all construction costs and all borrower-incurred fees and costs.
3. In a sale transaction, the deed from seller to buyer is recorded, and the seller is paid off. In a refinance, the previous mortgage is satisfied, and the new mortgage is recorded and funded. At this point, the title policy is realized.
4. In order to close concurrently on a loan, sources must include borrower's earnest money and down payment. The borrower's cash to close is also required and the borrower must pre-pay credit report fees and appraisal deposit. The loan proceeds are used to payoff or refinance the land, provide a credit to the seller (if any) for pre-paid taxes, escrow deposits for taxes and insurance. All funds are accounted for on the Closing Disclosure.
5. A promissory note indicates the borrower's promise to pay, and because it is a negotiable instrument, it is returned to the lender for safekeeping. The mortgage secures the promise to pay, and it is recorded in the county where the property is located.

Module 5

1. In the post-closing phase, the lender is responsible for ordering and reviewing progress inspections, collecting mechanic's lien waivers and/or ordering mechanic's lien endorsements, monitoring expiration dates on licenses and insurance and disbursing construction proceeds.
2. The first draw requires the following documents: permits, builder's risk insurance, draw request, survey and/or foundation endorsement, mechanic's lien waiver, progress inspection, architectural approval
3. When a lender replaces an original builder, several risks can occur:
   a) The exiting builder can lien the property if owed amounts are not paid.
   b) Finding a replacement builder can be difficult due to potential pre-existing construction defects where they could be held liable.
   c) A new builder may be hesitant to complete the construction for the amount of undisbursed funds remaining in the construction loan.
4. Prior to releasing the final draw, a lender must require a final progress inspection and a written statement from the borrower. If the municipality where the property is located requires a certificate of occupancy, the lender will also want a copy.
5. Troubled assets are those which fail to perform according to the terms of the note, the mortgage and the construction loan agreement. They also have the potential of causing financial losses to the lender.

Sample Reports and Forms

TRINITY
Loan Administration, LLC

Borrower Name:	Loan Number:	Bank / Mortgage Company:
Borrower – Property Address:	City, State, Zip Code	**Business Classification**
Legal Name of Company (Contractor):	Phone Number: ( ) -	Corporation ☐
Mailing address:	City, State, Zip Code	Partnership - General ☐ Limited Liability ☐
Website address, if applicable: www.		Sole Proprietorship ☐

1. Organization has been in business as a general contractor for _____ years.
   The primary geographic location for construction projects has been _____.

2. Type of license or "NONE REQUIRED":	License number:	Tax ID# (Required):

3. Organization has been in business under its present name for _____ years.
   Previous Business Name(s) (if any) _____

4. If organization is a corporation or LLC, complete this section.

Date of Incorporation:	☐ "C" Corp or ☐ "S" Corp ☐ LLC	State of Incorporation:

5. Name, Title, SSN and Ownership % of each partner, shareholder or member

Name	Title	Social Security Number	Ownership %
		- -	
		- -	
		- -	
		- -	

6. Insurance coverage

Liability Insurance $	Agent	Phone #
Workers Compensation $	Agent	Phone #

☐ If checked, I certify that my organization does not carry workers compensation insurance, because my organization does not have any field employees (other than myself), and all hired subcontractors are required to carry their own Workers Compensation insurance.

7. Has the organization or any of its principals ever filed bankruptcy?   Yes ☐   No ☐   If yes, give date and attach explanation.

8. I/We the undersigned certify that the statements and representations made herein are true and complete to the best of our knowledge. Should there be any personal or corporate changes within the company, I/we agree to notify lender of same within thirty (30) days thereof. I/We hereby acknowledge to have read the Disclosure and FCRA Summary of Rights located in Appendix A and authorize Trinity Loan Administration to obtain business and/or personal credit reports, and verify the information represented herein with employees, financial institutions, trade and customer references, and others as it may deem necessary or appropriate in its sole discretion. Certain credit and proprietary information of builder supplied to Trinity Loan Administration may be needed by Trinity Loan Administration in connection with the processing and underwriting of loans or projects involving the undersigned builder. Builder hereby consents to Trinity Loan Administration sharing such information, including business and personal credit reports, forms 1003 and 1008, tax returns, financial statements, account and other financial information, prior experience, construction industry reports and references, and other builder information, regardless of whether such information was first furnished to or obtained by Trinity Loan Administration.

Owner/Partner/Member	Title	Date
Owner/Partner/Member	Title	Date
Owner/Partner/Member	Title	Date

Draw Request / Direct Disbursement / Interim All Bill's Paid Affidavit

LOAN #: _____   Borrower: _____

Property Address: _____

APPLICATION IS MADE FOR PAYMENT AS SHOWN BELOW IN CONNECTION WITH THE ABOVE REFERENCED LOAN:

Current Draw Request $_____   **FINAL DRAW REQUEST   YES_____   NO_____**

General Contractor/Builder and Borrower state that all of the funds that are requested in the "Draw Request" will be used to pay for the labor and materials which created the improvements to the subject property. General Contractor/Builder and Borrower further state that all funds advanced before the date of this request (if any) were also used to pay for labor and materials for the improvements of the subject property. Borrower and General Contractor/Builder also state that the improvements completed to the subject property were completed as per the "Plans and Specifications" original submitted to the Lender, except for any "Change Orders" submitted to the Lender.

All disbursement requests must be submitted on a "Draw Request / Direct Disbursement / All Bill's Paid Affidavit." (Always place punctuation inside end quotes)

1. **Description of Transaction:** Borrower has a loan with _____, the "**Lender,**" to construct improvements on the property. Borrower owns the property. Borrower entered into a Contract of Improvements with Contractor to construct improvements on the referenced property. Lender would not have made the loan without Borrower's and Contractor's agreement to sign this Affidavit. The signatures on this Affidavit are genuine and the person or entity named has authority to sign this Affidavit.

2. **Contractor's and Borrower's Statement as to Debts of Liens:** Contractor and Borrower state that all of the funds that Lender has advanced before the date of this Affidavit (if any), have been used to pay for the labor and materials which have created the improvements on the Property. Contractor and Borrower state that there are no disputes with, or debts owed to, any mechanics, material men or subcontractors for the labor or materials furnished. There are no security interests or liens encumbering the Property other than those created in favor of Lender.

Amount ($) Quoted	Name of Vendor	Description of Completed Work	Amount ($) Requested
		TOTAL:	

3. **Funds Requested:** All of the work for which payment is requested in this Draw Request has been fully completed in a satisfactory and workmanlike manner and in compliance with all applicable building codes and other requirements. (this was a different font, so I aligned it with the remainder of the page)

4. **Funds Disbursed:** A portion of the funds available under the Loan to improve the Property are being disbursed this date in accordance with the terms of the loan documents, by Lender to the Contractor or to the Contractor and Borrower, less any Retainage held according to Lien Law.

5. **Retainage:** Borrower and Contractor requested Lender to hold Retainage (if any), equal to an amount defined in the Construction Loan Agreement.   Retainage will be released jointly to the Contractor and Borrower when the construction is 100% complete and all final documentation requirements defined in the Construction Loan Agreement have been met.

6. **Release:** Borrower and Contractor have made an inspection of the Property and hereby release and forever discharge Lender from any and all claims and actions which the Borrower and Contractor have or may have, whether known or unknown, past, present or future, arising from or based upon (1) the loan or (2) the construction of the improvements now located on the subject Property or (3) from any expressed or implied warranties relating to the improvements, including any implied warranties of merchantability, habitability, fitness for a particular purpose, or other warranties.

7. **Bankruptcy:** There is no pending bankruptcy proceeding naming Contractor or Borrower as a part. Neither Borrower nor Contractor has made any assignment for the benefit of creditors. Borrower and Contractor

acknowledge that bankruptcy of the persons or entities that sign this Affidavit will not discharge any liability owed to Lender which arises out of false statements made in this affidavit.

8. **Default:** Borrower and contractor certify there has been no event that has occurred through the date of this request that results in either a default or breach of agreement within the executed loan documents.

9. **Execution of Affidavit:** This affidavit has been jointly made by Borrower and Contractor or by and through an authorized representative of each, the same being the undersigned affiant, and may be recorded by any person with the county clerk of the county in which the Property is located, whereupon it shall be deemed to have been jointly filed by Borrower and Contractor.

The person(s) signing this Affidavit is/are personally liable for any loss or damage resulting from any false or incorrect information given on this form.

CONTRACTOR: BORROWER:

_____   _____
Name   Date   Name   Date

By: _____   By: _____
Signature   Date   Signature   Date

Its:_____
Title

Contractor Permit Advisory
(To be completed by Contractor)

Are permits required for the proposed scope of work? Yes? ☐   No ☐

If YES, please complete the following, sign and date, and send back to the tla@trinityonline.com with all other contractor documents.
`If NO, please sign, date and send back to the tla@trinityonline.com with all other contractor documents.

Permitting Entity Name: _____

Permit Office Address: _____

Permit Office Contact Name: _____

Permit Office Phone Number: _____

Permit Office Email Address: _____

Time to obtain all permits after application submitted: _____days

Time to complete the entire project, including permits: _____ days (This will be the "time to complete" that will be used on all project documentation.)

Contractor Initials:

_____ In order to receive the initial draw, a copy of the actual permit MUST be supplied.

_____ Contractor certifies that they are not related to the borrower in any way.

Contractor Signature: _____   Date: _____

Contractor Name: _____

Title: _____

Mechanic's Lien Affidavit

DATE: _____

BORROWER: _____

LOAN #: _____

PROPERTY ADDRESS: _____

STATE OF: _____

COUNTY OF: _____

Before me, the undersigned authority personally appeared (name) _____

Who being by me first duly sworn on oath say:

☐   1.   That the above described property is owned by the undersigned:

☐   2.   That the above described property is free and clear of all liens, taxes, assessments, encumbrances and claims of every kind, nature and description whatsoever, except for real estate taxes which are not now due and payable.

☐   3.   That there have been no improvements, alterations, or repairs to the above property involving work or materials for which the costs thereof remain unpaid, except (write "NONE" if applicable):

_____

☐   4.   That there are no mechanic's, materials men's or labors' liens against the above described property.

☐   5.   That the undersigned know(s) of no violations of municipal ordinances pertaining to the above described property.

☐   6.   That this affidavit is made for the purpose of inducing: _____

_____

Only those portions of this affidavit marked "X" are applicable to this affidavit.

_____   _____
Contractor's Signature   Date

Unconditional Waiver and Release on Progress Payment

Project: _____

Job No: _____

Loan No: _____

    The undersigned has been paid and has received a progress payment in the sum of $_____ for all labor, services, equipment or material furnished to the jobsite or to _____ on the job of_____located at _____, and does hereby release any mechanic's lien, any state or federal statutory bond right, any private bond right, any claim for payment and any rights under any similar ordinance, rule or statue related to claim or payment rights for persons in the undersigned's position that the undersigned has on the above referenced project to the following extent. This release covers a progress payment for all labor, services; equipment or materials furnished to the jobsite or to _____ through _____(date) only and does cover any retention, pending modifications and changes or items furnished after that date.

    The undersigned warrants that the below person/company either has already paid or will use the monies received from this progress payment to promptly pay in full all laborers, subcontractors, materialman and suppliers for all work, materials equipment or services provided for or to the above referenced project up to the date of this wavier.

Dated: _____

Contractor: _____

By: _____

Name: _____

Title: _____

NOTICE: THIS DOCUMENT WAIVES RIGHTS UNCONDITIONALLY AND STATES THAT YOU HAVE BEEN PAID FOR GIVING UP THOSE RIGHTS. THIS DOCUMENT IS ENFORCEABLE AGAINST YOU IF YOU SIGN IT, EVEN IF YOU HAVE NOT BEEN PAID. IF YOU HAVE NOT BEEN PAID, USE A CONDITIONAL RELEASE FORM.

Unconditional Waiver and Release on Final Payment

Project: _____

Job No: _____

Loan No: _____

     The undersigned has been paid in full for all labor, services, equipment or material furnished to the jobsite or to_____, on the job of _____ located at _____, and does hereby waive and release any right to any mechanic's lien, any state or federal statutory bond right, any private bond right, any claim for repayment and any rights under any similar ordinance, rule or statue related to claim or payment rights for persons in the undersigned's position, except for disputed claims for extra work in the amount of $_____.

     The undersigned warrants that the below person/company either has already paid or will use the monies received from this progress payment to promptly pay in full all laborers, subcontractors, materialman (is this a word? I don't find it in dictionary.com) and suppliers for all work, materials, equipment or services provided for or to the above referenced project.

Dated: _____

Contractor: _____

By: _____

Name: _____

Title: _____

NOTICE: THIS DOCUMENT WAIVES RIGHTS UNCONDITIONALLY AND STATES THAT YOU HAVE BEEN PAID FOR GIVING UP THOSE RIGHTS. THIS DOCUMENT IS ENFORCEABLE AGAINST YOU IF YOU SIGN IT, EVEN IF YOU HAVE NOT BEEN PAID. IF YOU HAVE NOT BEEN PAID, USE A CONDITIONAL RELEASE FORM.

Uniform Residential Appraisal Report   File

The purpose of this summary appraisal report is to provide the lender/client with an accurate, and adequately supported, opinion of the market value of the subject property.

Property Address	City	State	Zip Code

SUBJECT

Borrower	Owner of Public Record	County

Legal Description

Assessor's Parcel #	Tax Year	R.E. Taxes $
Neighborhood Name	Map Reference	Census Tract

Occupant ☐ Owner ☐ Tenant ☐ Vacant   Special Assessments $ ☐ PUD HOA $ ☐ per year ☐ per month

Property Rights Appraised ☐ Fee Simple ☐ Leasehold ☐ Other (describe)

Assignment Type ☐ Purchase Transaction ☐ Refinance Transaction ☐ Other (describe)

Lender/Client   Address

Is the subject property currently offered for sale or has it been offered for sale in the twelve months prior to the effective date of this appraisal? ☐ Yes ☐ No

Report data source(s) used, offering price(s), and date(s).

CONTRACT

I ☐ did ☐ did not analyze the contract for sale for the subject purchase transaction. Explain the results of the analysis of the contract for sale or why the analysis was not performed.

Contract Price $ Date of Contract   Is the property seller the owner of public record? ☐ Yes ☐ No Data Source(s)

Is there any financial assistance (loan charges, sale concessions, gift or downpayment assistance, etc.) to be paid by any party on behalf of the borrower? ☐ Yes ☐ No

If Yes, report the total dollar amount and describe the items to be paid.

NEIGHBORHOOD

Note: Race and the racial composition of the neighborhood are not appraisal factors.

Neighborhood Characteristics	One-Unit Housing Trends	One-Unit Housing	Present Land Use %
Location ☐ Urban ☐ Suburban ☐ Rural	Property Values ☐ Increasing ☐ Stable ☐ Declining	PRICE AGE	One-Unit %
Built-Up ☐ Over 75% ☐ 25–75% ☐ Under 25%	Demand/Supply ☐ Shortage ☐ In Balance ☐ Over Supply	$ (000) (yrs)	2-4 Unit %
Growth ☐ Rapid ☐ Stable ☐ Slow	Marketing Time ☐ Under 3 mths ☐ 3–6 mths ☐ Over 6 mths	Low	Multi-Family %
Neighborhood Boundaries		High	Commercial %
		Pred.	Other %

Neighborhood Description

Market Conditions (including support for the above conclusions)

SITE

Dimensions	Area	Shape	View

Specific Zoning Classification   Zoning Description

Zoning Compliance ☐ Legal ☐ Legal Nonconforming (Grandfathered Use) ☐ No Zoning ☐ Illegal (describe)

Is the highest and best use of the subject property as improved (or as proposed per plans and specifications) the present use? ☐ Yes ☐ No If No, describe

Utilities	Public	Other (describe)		Public	Other (describe)	Off-site Improvements—Type	Public	Private
Electricity	☐	☐	Water	☐	☐	Street	☐	☐
Gas	☐	☐	Sanitary Sewer	☐	☐	Alley	☐	☐

FEMA Special Flood Hazard Area ☐ Yes ☐ No FEMA Flood Zone   FEMA Map #   FEMA Map Date

Are the utilities and off-site improvements typical for the market area? ☐ Yes ☐ No If No, describe

Are there any adverse site conditions or external factors (easements, encroachments, environmental conditions, land uses, etc.)? ☐ Yes ☐ No If Yes, describe

IMPROVEMENTS

General Description	Foundation	Exterior Description materials/condition	Interior materials/condition
Units ☐ One ☐ One with Accessory Unit	☐ Concrete Slab ☐ Crawl Space	Foundation Walls	Floors
# of Stories	☐ Full Basement ☐ Partial Basement	Exterior Walls	Walls
Type ☐ Det. ☐ Att. ☐ S-Det./End Unit	Basement Area sq. ft.	Roof Surface	Trim/Finish
☐ Existing ☐ Proposed ☐ Under Const.	Basement Finish %	Gutters & Downspouts	Bath Floor
Design (Style)	☐ Outside Entry/Exit ☐ Sump Pump	Window Type	Bath Wainscot
Year Built	Evidence of ☐ Infestation	Storm Sash/Insulated	Car Storage ☐ None
Effective Age (Yrs)	☐ Dampness ☐ Settlement	Screens	☐ Driveway # of Cars
Attic ☐ None	Heating ☐ FWA ☐ HWBB ☐ Radiant	Amenities ☐ Woodstove(s) #	Driveway Surface
☐ Drop Stair ☐ Stairs	☐ Other Fuel	☐ Fireplace(s) # ☐ Fence	☐ Garage # of Cars
☐ Floor ☐ Scuttle	Cooling ☐ Central Air Conditioning	☐ Patio/Deck ☐ Porch	☐ Carport # of Cars
☐ Finished ☐ Heated	☐ Individual ☐ Other	☐ Pool ☐ Other	☐ Att. ☐ Det. ☐ Built-in

Appliances ☐ Refrigerator ☐ Range/Oven ☐ Dishwasher ☐ Disposal ☐ Microwave ☐ Washer/Dryer ☐ Other (describe)

Finished area **above** grade contains: Rooms   Bedrooms   Bath(s)   Square Feet of Gross Living Area Above Grade

Additional features (special energy efficient items, etc.)

Describe the condition of the property (including needed repairs, deterioration, renovations, remodeling, etc.).

Are there any physical deficiencies or adverse conditions that affect the livability, soundness, or structural integrity of the property? ☐ Yes ☐ No If Yes, describe

Does the property generally conform to the neighborhood (functional utility, style, condition, use, construction, etc.)? ☐ Yes ☐ No If No, describe

There are	comparable properties currently offered for sale in the subject neighborhood ranging in price from $		to $	
There are	comparable sales in the subject neighborhood within the past twelve months ranging in sale price from $		to $	

FEATURE	SUBJECT	COMPARABLE SALE # 1		COMPARABLE SALE # 2		COMPARABLE SALE # 3	
Address							
Proximity to Subject							
Sale Price	$		$		$		$
Sale Price/Gross Liv. Area	$ sq. ft.	$ sq. ft.		$ sq. ft.		$ sq. ft.	
Data Source(s)							
Verification Source(s)							
VALUE ADJUSTMENTS	DESCRIPTION	DESCRIPTION	+(-) $ Adjustment	DESCRIPTION	+(-) $ Adjustment	DESCRIPTION	+(-) $ Adjustment
Sale or Financing Concessions							
Date of Sale/Time							
Location							
Leasehold/Fee Simple							
Site							
View							
Design (Style)							
Quality of Construction							
Actual Age							
Condition							
Above Grade Room Count	Total | Bdrms. | Baths	Total | Bdrms. | Baths		Total | Bdrms. | Baths		Total | Bdrms. | Baths	
Gross Living Area	sq. ft.	sq. ft.		sq. ft.		sq. ft.	
Basement & Finished Rooms Below Grade							
Functional Utility							
Heating/Cooling							
Energy Efficient Items							
Garage/Carport							
Porch/Patio/Deck							
Net Adjustment (Total)		☐ + ☐ -	$	☐ + ☐ -	$	☐ + ☐ -	$
Adjusted Sale Price of Comparables		Net Adj. % Gross Adj. %	$	Net Adj. % Gross Adj. %	$	Net Adj. % Gross Adj. %	$

I ☐ did ☐ did not research the sale or transfer history of the subject property and comparable sales. If not, explain

My research ☐ did ☐ did not reveal any prior sales or transfers of the subject property for the three years prior to the effective date of this appraisal.

Data source(s)

My research ☐ did ☐ did not reveal any prior sales or transfers of the comparable sales for the year prior to the date of sale of the comparable sale.

Data source(s)

Report the results of the research and analysis of the prior sale or transfer history of the subject property and comparable sales (report additional prior sales on page 3).

ITEM	SUBJECT	COMPARABLE SALE # 1	COMPARABLE SALE # 2	COMPARABLE SALE # 3
Date of Prior Sale/Transfer				
Price of Prior Sale/Transfer				
Data Source(s)				
Effective Date of Data Source(s)				

Analysis of prior sale or transfer history of the subject property and comparable sales

Summary of Sales Comparison Approach

Indicated Value by Sales Comparison Approach $

Indicated Value by: Sales Comparison Approach $ Cost Approach (if developed) $ Income Approach (if developed) $

This appraisal is made ☐ "as is", ☐ subject to completion per plans and specifications on the basis of a hypothetical condition that the improvements have been completed, ☐ subject to the following repairs or alterations on the basis of a hypothetical condition that the repairs or alterations have been completed, or ☐ subject to the following required inspection based on the extraordinary assumption that the condition or deficiency does not require alteration or repair:

Based on a complete visual inspection of the interior and exterior areas of the subject property, defined scope of work, statement of assumptions and limiting conditions, and appraiser's certification, my (our) opinion of the market value, as defined, of the real property that is the subject of this report is
$, as of   , which is the date of inspection and the effective date of this appraisal.

Uniform Residential Appraisal Report

File #

ADDITIONAL COMMENTS

COST APPROACH TO VALUE (not required by Fannie Mae)

Provide adequate information for the lender/client to replicate the below cost figures and calculations.

Support for the opinion of site value (summary of comparable land sales or other methods for estimating site value)

COST APPROACH

ESTIMATED ☐ REPRODUCTION OR ☐ REPLACEMENT COST NEW | OPINION OF SITE VALUE .... = $

Source of cost data | Dwelling | Sq. Ft. @ $ | .... =$

Quality rating from cost service   Effective date of cost data | | Sq. Ft. @ $ | .... =$

Comments on Cost Approach (gross living area calculations, depreciation, etc.)

| | Garage/Carport | Sq. Ft. @ $ | .... =$
| | Total Estimate of Cost-New | .... = $
| | Less | Physical | Functional | External |
| | Depreciation | | | | =$( )
| | Depreciated Cost of Improvements....................................... =$
| | "As-is" Value of Site Improvements.. =$

Estimated Remaining Economic Life (HUD and VA only)   Years | Indicated Value By Cost Approach .... =$

INCOME APPROACH TO VALUE (not required by Fannie Mae)

INCOME

Estimated Monthly Market Rent $ _____ X Gross Rent Multiplier _____ = $ _____ Indicated Value by Income Approach

Summary of Income Approach (including support for market rent and GRM)

PROJECT INFORMATION FOR PUDs (if applicable)

PUD INFORMATION

Is the developer/builder in control of the Homeowners' Association (HOA)? ☐ Yes ☐ No   Unit type(s) ☐ Detached ☐ Attached

Provide the following information for PUDs ONLY if the developer/builder is in control of the HOA and the subject property is an attached dwelling unit.

Legal name of project

Total number of phases _____ Total number of units _____ Total number of units sold _____

Total number of units rented _____ Total number of units for sale _____ Data source(s)

Was the project created by the conversion of an existing building(s) into a PUD? ☐ Yes ☐ No   If Yes, date of conversion

Does the project contain any multi-dwelling units? ☐ Yes ☐ No   Data source(s)

Are the units, common elements, and recreation facilities complete? ☐ Yes ☐ No   If No, describe the status of completion.

Are the common elements leased to or by the Homeowners' Association? ☐ Yes ☐ No   If Yes, describe the rental terms and options.

Describe common elements and recreational facilities

Freddie Mac Form 70   March 2005

Page 3 of 6

Fannie Mae Form 1004   March 2005

Uniform Residential Appraisal Report File

This report form is designed to report an appraisal of a one-unit property or a one-unit property with an accessory unit; including a unit in a planned unit development (PUD). This report form is not designed to report an appraisal of a manufactured home or a unit in a condominium or cooperative project.

This appraisal report is subject to the following scope of work, intended use, intended user, definition of market value, statement of assumptions and limiting conditions, and certifications. Modifications, additions, or deletions to the intended use, intended user, definition of market value, or assumptions and limiting conditions are not permitted. The appraiser may expand the scope of work to include any additional research or analysis necessary based on the complexity of this appraisal assignment. Modifications or deletions to the certifications are also not permitted. However, additional certifications that do not constitute material alterations to this appraisal report, such as those required by law or those related to the appraiser's continuing education or membership in an appraisal organization, are permitted.

SCOPE OF WORK: The scope of work for this appraisal is defined by the complexity of this appraisal assignment and the reporting requirements of this appraisal report form, including the following definition of market value, statement of assumptions and limiting conditions, and certifications. The appraiser must, at a minimum: (1) perform a complete visual inspection of the interior and exterior areas of the subject property, (2) inspect the neighborhood, (3) inspect each of the comparable sales from at least the street, (4) research, verify, and analyze data from reliable public and/or private sources, and (5) report his or her analysis, opinions, and conclusions in this appraisal report.

INTENDED USE: The intended use of this appraisal report is for the lender/client to evaluate the property that is the subject of this appraisal for a mortgage finance transaction.

INTENDED USER: The intended user of this appraisal report is the lender/client.

DEFINITION OF MARKET VALUE: The most probable price which a property should bring in a competitive and open market under all conditions requisite to a fair sale, the buyer and seller, each acting prudently, knowledgeably and assuming the price is not affected by undue stimulus. Implicit in this definition is the consummation of a sale as of a specified date and the passing of title from seller to buyer under conditions whereby: (1) buyer and seller are typically motivated; (2) both parties are well informed or well advised, and each acting in what he or she considers his or her own best interest; (3) a reasonable time is allowed for exposure in the open market; (4) payment is made in terms of cash in U. S. dollars or in terms of financial arrangements comparable thereto; and (5) the price represents the normal consideration for the property sold unaffected by special or creative financing or sales concessions* granted by anyone associated with the sale.

*Adjustments to the comparables must be made for special or creative financing or sales concessions. No adjustments are necessary for those costs which are normally paid by sellers as a result of tradition or law in a market area; these costs are readily identifiable since the seller pays these costs in virtually all sales transactions. Special or creative financing adjustments can be made to the comparable property by comparisons to financing terms offered by a third party institutional lender that is not already involved in the property or transaction. Any adjustment should not be calculated on a mechanical dollar for dollar cost of the financing or concession but the dollar amount of any adjustment should approximate the market's reaction to the financing or concessions based on the appraiser's judgment.

STATEMENT OF ASSUMPTIONS AND LIMITING CONDITIONS: The appraiser's certification in this report is subject to the following assumptions and limiting conditions:

1. The appraiser will not be responsible for matters of a legal nature that affect either the property being appraised or the title to it, except for information that he or she became aware of during the research involved in performing this appraisal. The appraiser assumes that the title is good and marketable and will not render any opinions about the title.

2. The appraiser has provided a sketch in this appraisal report to show the approximate dimensions of the improvements. The sketch is included only to assist the reader in visualizing the property and understanding the appraiser's determination of its size.

3. The appraiser has examined the available flood maps that are provided by the Federal Emergency Management Agency (or other data sources) and has noted in this appraisal report whether any portion of the subject site is located in an identified Special Flood Hazard Area. Because the appraiser is not a surveyor, he or she makes no guarantees, express or implied, regarding this determination.

4. The appraiser will not give testimony or appear in court because he or she made an appraisal of the property in question, unless specific arrangements to do so have been made beforehand, or as otherwise required by law.

5. The appraiser has noted in this appraisal report any adverse conditions (such as needed repairs, deterioration, the presence of hazardous wastes, toxic substances, etc.) observed during the inspection of the subject property or that he or she became aware of during the research involved in performing this appraisal. Unless otherwise stated in this appraisal report, the appraiser has no knowledge of any hidden or unapparent physical deficiencies or adverse conditions of the property (such as, but not limited to, needed repairs, deterioration, the presence of hazardous wastes, toxic substances, adverse environmental conditions, etc.) that would make the property less valuable, and has assumed that there are no such conditions and makes no guarantees or warranties, express or implied. The appraiser will not be responsible for any such conditions that do exist or for any engineering or testing that might be required to discover whether such conditions exist. Because the appraiser is not an expert in the field of environmental hazards, this appraisal report must not be considered as an environmental assessment of the property.

6. The appraiser has based his or her appraisal report and valuation conclusion for an appraisal that is subject to satisfactory completion, repairs, or alterations on the assumption that the completion, repairs, or alterations of the subject property will be performed in a professional manner.

Uniform Residential Appraisal Report File

APPRAISER'S CERTIFICATION: The Appraiser certifies and agrees that:

1. I have, at a minimum, developed and reported this appraisal in accordance with the scope of work requirements stated in this appraisal report.

2. I performed a complete visual inspection of the interior and exterior areas of the subject property. I reported the condition of the improvements in factual, specific terms. I identified and reported the physical deficiencies that could affect the livability, soundness, or structural integrity of the property.

3. I performed this appraisal in accordance with the requirements of the Uniform Standards of Professional Appraisal Practice that were adopted and promulgated by the Appraisal Standards Board of The Appraisal Foundation and that were in place at the time this appraisal report was prepared.

4. I developed my opinion of the market value of the real property that is the subject of this report based on the sales comparison approach to value. I have adequate comparable market data to develop a reliable sales comparison approach for this appraisal assignment. I further certify that I considered the cost and income approaches to value but did not develop them, unless otherwise indicated in this report.

5. I researched, verified, analyzed, and reported on any current agreement for sale for the subject property, any offering for sale of the subject property in the twelve months prior to the effective date of this appraisal, and the prior sales of the subject property for a minimum of three years prior to the effective date of this appraisal, unless otherwise indicated in this report.

6. I researched, verified, analyzed, and reported on the prior sales of the comparable sales for a minimum of one year prior to the date of sale of the comparable sale, unless otherwise indicated in this report.

7. I selected and used comparable sales that are locationally, physically, and functionally the most similar to the subject property.

8. I have not used comparable sales that were the result of combining a land sale with the contract purchase price of a home that has been built or will be built on the land.

9. I have reported adjustments to the comparable sales that reflect the market's reaction to the differences between the subject property and the comparable sales.

10. I verified, from a disinterested source, all information in this report that was provided by parties who have a financial interest in the sale or financing of the subject property.

11. I have knowledge and experience in appraising this type of property in this market area.

12. I am aware of, and have access to, the necessary and appropriate public and private data sources, such as multiple listing services, tax assessment records, public land records and other such data sources for the area in which the property is located.

13. I obtained the information, estimates, and opinions furnished by other parties and expressed in this appraisal report from reliable sources that I believe to be true and correct.

14. I have taken into consideration the factors that have an impact on value with respect to the subject neighborhood, subject property, and the proximity of the subject property to adverse influences in the development of my opinion of market value. I have noted in this appraisal report any adverse conditions (such as, but not limited to, needed repairs, deterioration, the presence of hazardous wastes, toxic substances, adverse environmental conditions, etc.) observed during the inspection of the subject property or that I became aware of during the research involved in performing this appraisal. I have considered these adverse conditions in my analysis of the property value, and have reported on the effect of the conditions on the value and marketability of the subject property.

15. I have not knowingly withheld any significant information from this appraisal report and, to the best of my knowledge, all statements and information in this appraisal report are true and correct.

16. I stated in this appraisal report my own personal, unbiased, and professional analysis, opinions, and conclusions, which are subject only to the assumptions and limiting conditions in this appraisal report.

17. I have no present or prospective interest in the property that is the subject of this report, and I have no present or prospective personal interest or bias with respect to the participants in the transaction. I did not base, either partially or completely, my analysis and/or opinion of market value in this appraisal report on the race, color, religion, sex, age, marital status, handicap, familial status, or national origin of either the prospective owners or occupants of the subject property or of the present owners or occupants of the properties in the vicinity of the subject property or on any other basis prohibited by law.

18. My employment and/or compensation for performing this appraisal or any future or anticipated appraisals was not conditioned on any agreement or understanding, written or otherwise, that I would report (or present analysis supporting) a predetermined specific value, a predetermined minimum value, a range or direction in value, a value that favors the cause of any party, or the attainment of a specific result or occurrence of a specific subsequent event (such as approval of a pending mortgage loan application).

19. I personally prepared all conclusions and opinions about the real estate that were set forth in this appraisal report. If I relied on significant real property appraisal assistance from any individual or individuals in the performance of this appraisal or the preparation of this appraisal report, I have named such individual(s) and disclosed the specific tasks performed in this appraisal report. I certify that any individual so named is qualified to perform the tasks. I have not authorized anyone to make a change to any item in this appraisal report; therefore, any change made to this appraisal is unauthorized and I will take no responsibility for it.

20. I identified the lender/client in this appraisal report who is the individual, organization, or agent for the organization that ordered and will receive this appraisal report.

Uniform Residential Appraisal Report

21. The lender/client may disclose or distribute this appraisal report to: the borrower; another lender at the request of the borrower; the mortgagee or its successors and assigns; mortgage insurers; government sponsored enterprises; other secondary market participants; data collection or reporting services; professional appraisal organizations; any department, agency, or instrumentality of the United States; and any state, the District of Columbia, or other jurisdictions; without having to obtain the appraiser's or supervisory appraiser's (if applicable) consent. Such consent must be obtained before this appraisal report may be disclosed or distributed to any other party (including, but not limited to, the public through advertising, public relations, news, sales, or other media).

22. I am aware that any disclosure or distribution of this appraisal report by me or the lender/client may be subject to certain laws and regulations. Further, I am also subject to the provisions of the Uniform Standards of Professional Appraisal Practice that pertain to disclosure or distribution by me.

23. The borrower, another lender at the request of the borrower, the mortgagee or its successors and assigns, mortgage insurers, government sponsored enterprises, and other secondary market participants may rely on this appraisal report as part of any mortgage finance transaction that involves any one or more of these parties.

24. If this appraisal report was transmitted as an "electronic record" containing my "electronic signature," as those terms are defined in applicable federal and/or state laws (excluding audio and video recordings), or a facsimile transmission of this appraisal report containing a copy or representation of my signature, the appraisal report shall be as effective, enforceable and valid as if a paper version of this appraisal report were delivered containing my original hand written signature.

25. Any intentional or negligent misrepresentation(s) contained in this appraisal report may result in civil liability and/or criminal penalties including, but not limited to, fine or imprisonment or both under the provisions of Title 18, United States Code, Section 1001, et seq., or similar state laws.

SUPERVISORY APPRAISER'S CERTIFICATION: The Supervisory Appraiser certifies and agrees that:

1. I directly supervised the appraiser for this appraisal assignment, have read the appraisal report, and agree with the appraiser's analysis, opinions, statements, conclusions, and the appraiser's certification.

2. I accept full responsibility for the contents of this appraisal report including, but not limited to, the appraiser's analysis, opinions, statements, conclusions, and the appraiser's certification.

3. The appraiser identified in this appraisal report is either a sub-contractor or an employee of the supervisory appraiser (or the appraisal firm), is qualified to perform this appraisal, and is acceptable to perform this appraisal under the applicable state law.

4. This appraisal report complies with the Uniform Standards of Professional Appraisal Practice that were adopted and promulgated by the Appraisal Standards Board of The Appraisal Foundation and that were in place at the time this appraisal report was prepared.

5. If this appraisal report was transmitted as an "electronic record" containing my "electronic signature," as those terms are defined in applicable federal and/or state laws (excluding audio and video recordings), or a facsimile transmission of this appraisal report containing a copy or representation of my signature, the appraisal report shall be as effective, enforceable and valid as if a paper version of this appraisal report were delivered containing my original hand written signature.

APPRAISER	SUPERVISORY APPRAISER (ONLY IF REQUIRED)
Signature_____	Signature_____
Name _____	Name _____
Company Name _____	Company Name _____
Company Address_____	Company Address_____
_____	_____
Telephone Number _____	Telephone Number _____
Email Address_____	Email Address_____
Date of Signature and Report_____	Date of Signature _____
Effective Date of Appraisal _____	State Certification # _____
State Certification #_____	or State License # _____
or State License # _____	State _____
or Other (describe) _____ State # _____	Expiration Date of Certification or License _____
State _____	
Expiration Date of Certification or License _____	SUBJECT PROPERTY
	☐ Did not inspect subject property
ADDRESS OF PROPERTY APPRAISED	☐ Did inspect exterior of subject property from street
_____	Date of Inspection _____
_____	☐ Did inspect interior and exterior of subject property
APPRAISED VALUE OF SUBJECT PROPERTY $ _____	Date of Inspection _____
LENDER/CLIENT	
Name _____	COMPARABLE SALES
Company Name _____	☐ Did not inspect exterior of comparable sales from street
Company Address_____	☐ Did inspect exterior of comparable sales from street
Email Address_____	Date of Inspection _____

Page 78

Instructions

Uniform Residential Appraisal Report

This report form is designed to report an appraisal of a one-unit property or a one-unit property with an accessory unit; including a unit in a planned unit development (PUD), based on an interior and exterior inspection of the subject property. This report form is not designed to report an appraisal of a manufactured home or a unit in a condominium or cooperative project.

Use

This report form is designed to report an appraisal of a one-unit property or a one-unit property with an accessory unit; including a unit in a planned unit development (PUD), based on an interior and exterior inspection of the subject property. This report form is not designed to report an appraisal of a manufactured home or a unit in a condominium or cooperative project.

Modifications, Additions, or Deletions

This appraisal report is subject to the scope of work, intended use, intended user, definition of market value, statement of assumptions and limiting conditions, and certifications contained in the report form. Modifications, additions, or deletions to the intended use, intended user, definition of market value, or assumptions and limiting conditions are not permitted. The appraiser may expand the scope of work to include any additional research or analysis necessary based on the complexity of this appraisal assignment. Modifications or deletions to the certifications are also not permitted. However, additional certifications that do not constitute material alterations to this appraisal report, such as those required by law or those related to the appraiser's continuing education or membership in an appraisal organization are permitted.

Scope of Work

The scope of work for this appraisal is defined by the complexity of this appraisal assignment and the reporting requirements of this appraisal report form, including the following definition of market value, statement of assumptions and limiting conditions, and certifications. The appraiser must, at a minimum: (1) perform a complete visual inspection of the interior and exterior areas of the subject property, (2) inspect the neighborhood, (3) inspect each of the comparable sales from at least the street, (4) research, verify, and analyze data from reliable public and/or private sources, and (5) report his or her analysis, opinions, and conclusions in this appraisal report.

Required Exhibits

- A street map that shows the location of the subject property and of all comparables that the appraiser used;

- An exterior building sketch of the improvements that indicates the dimensions. The appraiser must also include calculations to show how he or she arrived at the estimate for gross living area. A floor plan sketch that indicates the dimensions is required instead of the exterior building or unit sketch if the floor plan is atypical or functionally obsolete, thus limiting the market appeal for the property in comparison to competitive properties in the neighborhood;

- Clear, descriptive photographs (either in black and white or color) that show the front, back, and a street scene of the subject property, and that are appropriately identified. (Photographs must be originals that are produced either by photography or electronic imaging.);

- Clear, descriptive photographs (either in black and white or color) that show the front of each comparable sale and that are appropriately identified. Generally, photographs should be originals that are produced by photography or electronic imaging; however, copies of photographs from a multiple listing service or from the appraiser's files are acceptable if they are clear and descriptive;

- Any other data--as an attachment or addendum to the appraisal report form--that are necessary to provide an adequately supported opinion of market value.

NOTES

NOTES

NOTES